# Edmonton *Heritage* Stories

A collection of stories on

crossings, courage,
community

*Our Dedication*

To all those dear to us – who inspire us to love, strive, dream, and overcome.

To all those who came before us – who opened doors and widened paths for us to dream and imagine a better future together.

EDMONTON HERITAGE STORIES:
*Crossings, Courage, Community*

Email inquiries to Edmonton Chinese Writing Club (ECWC),
ecwc.ab@yahoo.com

*Book Project Manager: Ying Shi*
*Book Project Team: Roxanne Riemer, Ting Pimentel-Elger*
*Guest Editor and Book Design: Mila Bongco-Philipzig*
*Editorial Team: Goldwin McEwen, Rong Guo*
*Cover and Section art: Eoshanelle Francisco*

Published by the Edmonton Chinese Writing Club, Edmonton, Canada

ISBN:
    Paperback   978-1-77354-652-0
        ebook   978-1-77354-659-9

Publication assistance by
PAGEMASTER
PUBLISHING
PageMaster.ca

# Edmonton *Heritage* Stories

A collection of stories on

crossings, courage, community

# Table of Contents

Jamie Laventure, "Bridge" Monoprint 2022

# Preface

THIS EXHILARATING VOLUME OF SHORT STORIES AND POEMS IS A RESULT of the project *Creative Writing Boot Camp: Sharing Wisdom Across Cultures through Stories*. It is a world wisdom book project, dedicated to capturing and sharing stories about Canada's rich cultural landscapes, natural history, built heritage, significant objects, and linguistic diversity. This book focuses on stories about Edmonton.

The Edmonton Chinese Writing Club (ECWC) is the organization behind the idea of publishing a book to promote and preserve Edmonton heritage. This book is based on storytelling from various members of many cultural communities in this city of Edmonton. An Edmonton Heritage Council grant provided the funding to make this vision a reality.

We are happy to have the guidance of experienced editors and other professional authors and poets to help local authors enhance their creative writing and public speaking skills, while contributing collectively to a book that reflects some of the diversity and depth of Edmonton's stories. This publication serves as a valuable resource for preserving and celebrating Edmonton's heritage. For more information about this project and the ECWC in general, please go to our website: https://ecwc-ab.com/.

Jamie Laventure, "Muttart" Monoprint

# Introduction

THIS BOOK PRESENTS STORIES WRITTEN BY OUR NEIGHBOURS AND friends. Ordinary people, guided by volunteer editors, created these stories and poems for you to enjoy. Their words are sincere, narrating authentic sentiments and experiences. The writing in this book expresses a love for Edmonton - a real affection for the people and the place. At the same time, there is awareness and recognition that we need to better understand the evolving definition of what it means to be Canadian for those who started from somewhere else.

For new and developing Canadians - newcomers, immigrants, and children of immigrants - there remains a continued attraction for our heritage countries to which one may be bound by history and family. Mostly, we develop a love big enough to straddle two worlds - this new place we start calling home, and the land, memories, and people from our past, as well as the legacies from our ancestors.

This book has been divided into five sections: 1) Inspired Beginnings, 2) Meaningful Connections, 3) Discovering Belonging, 4) My Roots, My Community, and 5) Awareness and Insights. Most immigrants and newcomers go through all of these five themes in their journey of adapting and adjusting in Canada. But the life journey as expressed by each writer here shows how each story or poem serves to highlight one of the five themes listed.

*Inspired Beginnings* is a very apt start to this book: the stories swing from Ryan Lacanilao's celebration of his son's birth in the McCauley neighborhood to Marvin Cao's story of deciding to leave Beijing and having to start all over with an Engineering degree at NAIT; to Cynthia Palmaria's move from Montreal to Edmonton for a new career, then to Oliver Rossier relating the story of his mom, Ulrike Rossier's recovery from an aneurysm to become the 2021 Artist of the Year for the Nina Haggerty Center.

From various perspectives, the works of Jesus Tigulo, Yanjian Luo, Manna Liu, and Rong Guo are included in the *Meaningful Connections* section. These stories expound on the difficulties of immigrants having to grapple with a new place, weather, and language, while delighting in discovering the bonds and bridges formed by making friends and finding a connection with the new city. The last piece is Rong Guo's powerful story written during China's one child policy which navigates family dynamics, and the difficult decisions and deep emotions surrounding having children.

When someone has more than one heritage background, the sense of belonging is fraught with  hardships and complexities. The next section, *Discovering Belonging*, shows the complications and nuances of belonging in the stories and poems from Goldwin McEwen, Paul Fujishige, Ting Pimentel-Elger, and Roxanne Riemer. *The History Lesson* from Paul Fujishige, for example, invites one to reflect on why have we not learned from the past to be inclusive and welcoming, instead of continuing to repeat mistakes of exclusion.

*My Roots, My Community* consists of five stories from various cultural perspectives on finding affirmation and strength from being actively involved in one's cultural communities. Launa Linaker, Pravatika Rai, William Wang, Dan Li, and Khrystyna Zalutska all provide captivating narratives and poems about fending off isolation and apprehensions by being rooted in their heritage, recognizing their ancestors, participating in community building, and appreciating city services like the ETS.

The concluding section is *Awareness and Insights*. Emily Tworek narrates how the story of her Bapci inspire and strengthen her to deal with challenging work situations and decisions. Mila Philipzig and Candice Joy Oliva write about love for land and nature, and question why Community Gardens are being overtaken by concrete. Ying Shi writes about her journey in seeking happiness and raising new awareness what happiness means. Wai-Ling Lennon, Wang Xu, and Yuzhen Li write about the cultural richness in Edmonton Chinatown, the beauty and inspiration in Chinese art, and the optimism and hope evoked by people and organizations actively keeping Chinatown and Chinese culture thriving in Edmonton.

This book is enhanced by artworks from The Nina Haggerty Centre, home to one of Edmonton's most interesting art collectives, made up entirely of artists with developmental disabilities. The Nina is a unique and precious presence in our city and its motto "Changing Lives through Art" also deeply resonate with the vision of this book project.

A city is not alive without its people. Where there are people, there are stories and art. Where there are stories and art, there are opportunities to learn from each other, and expand our knowledge and experiences.

May this anthology make you more curious about your neighbors and your city and inspire you to be more connected with them.

# inspired beginnings

"The secret to a rich life is to have more beginnings than endings." - David Weinbaum

# McCauley

**By Ryan Lacanilao**

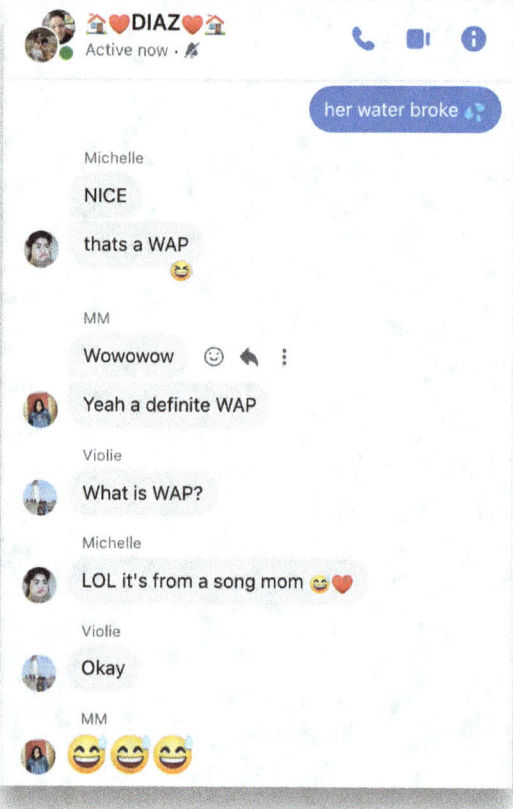

I SHOWED MARIELLE HER FAMILY GROUP CHAT, AND SHE LOL'D AS SHE adjusted her too-big gown, white with a snowflake pattern.

"Should I answer what a WAP is?" I started typing: w…e…t…

"No!" Marielle sat up in her narrow bed that bent in the middle like an open flip phone. Her squinting eyes curled up in the corners, betraying the smile hidden behind a mandatory face mask.

We weren't far from home. According to Google Maps, the Royal Alexandra Hospital is only an eight-minute walk from our house in McCauley. The day before, we told the doula we'd walk, and she shut that idea down fast, saying it would be hard enough for Marielle to walk eight steps after having a baby.

\* \* \*

When we moved to McCauley four months earlier, we liked how close it was to the downtown core. It's home to some of the city's best events, like Togather Chinatown Arts Festival and Heart of the City Music and Arts Festival. We've since met our welcoming neighbours at our community league get-togethers, and there's a wonderful sense of community. I love the gigantic trees that line the streets—it's one of Edmonton's oldest neighbourhoods. Our house is right between Chinatown and Little Italy. It was built in 1912, so it lived through the transition from horse to car, the Great Depression, and two world wars. It would be an honour to live in a place with so much history, to create our own there.

The Edmonton Journal created an ethnic map that showed the Filipino community is "concentrated on the edge of Edmonton, in places like MacEwan, Tamarack and Lewis Estates," which would explain why I've only seen one other Filipino family at McCauley community events. There's a stigma to the neighbourhood. At a comedy show in the neighbourhood, a Filipino comedian joked that people will be missing their bikes and cars by the end of the show. The municipal census found McCauley to be the lowest income neighbourhood in the city. Every day I see unhoused people walking by some still and hunched over from using something called the "zombie drug." Walking by needles and condoms on the sidewalk is just a normal Tuesday. I remember the night a cop was using the hood of my car as a surface to write, and I later found out someone had been murdered on our sidewalk.

We moved to McCauley when Marielle was five months pregnant. A friend asked me, "Why would you choose to raise a kid there?"

"I don't want my kid to grow up being scared of unhoused folks," I said. "I want them to be comfortable around people of all socioeconomic levels. I don't want them to be sheltered from reality. When it comes to cities—or people—when you see and appreciate the less savoury parts, the struggles, the pain, that's when you *really* appreciate them."

* * *

With Marielle in labour, It came in handy to be a few blocks from the biggest and busiest hospital in Western Canada—it also has the Louis Hole Hospital for Women with the specialists needed to handle high risk births. We were in a fourth-floor room that had a curtain as a wall. The baby had the umbilical cord wrapped around his neck twice, so the night before, they did a stress test to see how he would tolerate delivery. A resident doctor pumped Marielle with oxytocin to induce contractions— if the baby fails, they schedule a c-section. Luckily, the baby passed, so the doctor stuck a gel patch on Marielle's cervix to ripen it, and we made the two-minute drive to spend the night at home.

Marielle had to have labour induced two weeks before the baby's due date because her OBGYN said the baby was experiencing growth restriction. They were concerned the baby wasn't getting enough nutrients from the placenta, so inducing early labour would be the safest option.

It was the morning after induction, back in the curtain-walled room in Assessment & Induction, and Marielle was in labour. An hour after the WAP texts, I sent an update text to our doula:

Me:     she's contracting every 2 minutes For a minute
        duration. she's 2-3cm dilated, 75% effaced, and -2 to -3
        station. they're admitting her

Two and a half hours later, things had escalated:

Me:     they found that the baby's heart rate is sometimes
        dropping during contractions, so they're concerned
        and continuously monitoring her now. they're
        wanting to put an iv in just in case something bad
        happens

        4cm dilated, 75% effaced, -2 to -3 station

Doula:  Okay, keep me posted! That cord!

We had taken doula classes to prepare for this day. In class, Marielle held ice cubes in her hand to induce pain, and we practiced what to do. I knew where to press when she was in pain. I knew my role, but now that unexpected complications were arising, I felt lost.

"Do you want an epidural?" the nurse asked.

"Not yet, I think I can still handle it." Marielle's breathing was getting heavier, her contractions longer. She breathed through the contractions with a steady grip on my hands.

After another half hour of active labour, the nurse said, "We can move you to Delivery now." She called a porter in, and he wheeled Marielle out of the curtain-walled room, down a bunch of halls, and into a room five times bigger with actual walls. A new nurse took over. She said Marielle could take off her face mask, and she stayed next to Marielle to help her through the contractions.

In the new room, I felt Marielle's grip falter. Her shoulders rose as she inhaled, then she whimpered through clenched jaws. She winced as she squeezed my hand, and I felt trembling in her grip.

"I'm ready for the epidural!" she said as she braced for the next contraction.

"The anesthesiologist just went into a c-section," the nurse said. "We can't give you an epidural now."

"Oh my god, will you be okay?" I asked.

Marielle shrugged and shook her head.

A doctor came in, and after assessing, he said the baby's heart rate is dangerously low, and if we're not able to get it to a safe level, they'll have to do an emergency c-section. The nurse coached Marielle through the breathing and squeezing, but the baby's heart rate wouldn't go up.

After about fifteen minutes, the nurse said, "I have an idea. Why don't you try going on your hands and knees?" Marielle flipped over just in time for the next contraction. After the contraction passed, the nurse said, "It worked! The baby's heart rate is up!"

Our doula arrived and took over coaching Marielle.

"Where are things at with the epidural?" Marielle asked.

"Sorry," the nurse said, "I don't think you'll be able to get one."

"Okay. I feel like pushing," Marielle said.

"Don't push yet, it's too early." The nurse checked Marielle's cervix just to be sure. "Never mind, you're at ten centimetres! Push!"

The doula, the nurse, and I cheered Marielle on as she pushed. The doctor came in and shot a little suction cup arrow into Marielle onto the baby's head. Marielle's entire body tensed, and she grunted as she pushed. The grunt became a scream at the end of every push.

"The baby's heart rate is too low," the doctor said. "You have to push the baby out right now!"

The nurse went from encouraging to stern. "This is it, Marielle! You have to get the baby out on the next push!"

"I can't!" Marielle's eyebrows furrowed and she shook her head in defeat.

"You have to!" the nurse said. She sounded angry. "You don't have a choice! Your baby can't go much longer. You have to do it. Now!"

Our doula glared at the nurse, then smiled at Marielle. "You got this, Marielle! You're so strong!"

Marielle took a huge breath, then everyone yelled, "Push!!!" as she put everything she had left into it.

"Aaaaaaaaah!" Marielle yelled as the baby's head popped out. The baby opened his eyes and looked around. Our doula told us that was the first time she ever saw a baby open their eyes and look around while their body was still inside.

After delivering the head, the rest of the baby wouldn't come out. The doctor told us the baby had shoulder dystocia—the baby's shoulder was caught above Marielle's pubic bone. If he was stuck for too long, the lack of oxygen would cause brain damage. After a few minutes, the doctor was able to rotate the baby in a maneuver that freed his shoulder.

The baby was out! I expected a cry, but the baby was silent. I expected to cut the umbilical cord, but they clamped it and cut it themselves. I expected them to give the baby to Marielle, but they rushed him over to the NICU team waiting to the side.

This was my first baby, so I didn't know exactly how things were supposed to go, but I knew something was wrong. Then, in all the commotion, I heard someone mention the baby wasn't breathing.

I froze. I felt the thuds of my heartbeat get faster and more intense as I sent a plea into the universe. I knew this was a defining moment.

The next minute went by in slow motion. The NICU team placed our baby on a table attached to a panel with a bunch of buttons, knobs, and gauges. There were wires and tubes coming from the panel. One of them held our baby while another shoved a tube down his throat. Seconds later, the tube came out, but our baby didn't make a sound.

* * *

"He looks good!" Someone from the NICU team broke the silence.

"Waaaaaaaahhhhh!" Our baby interrupted.

"He looks great! Would you like him on your chest?" they asked Marielle.

Marielle nodded, and they brought our baby over to her.

"Thank god he's cute," Marielle said. She had been worried that freshly born babies look gross. Our baby stopped crying as she cuddled him. "So are you going to stitch me up?" she asked the doctor.

"I already did," he said.

Once the doctors and nurses left and it was just our little family and our doula left, Marielle went to the washroom. She stayed in the washroom for an hour and later told me that her post-delivery pee was more painful than the actual delivery.

As she tried to pee, I cradled our baby in my arms. I wrapped the blankie around him and rocked him, looked at him, kissed him. He freed his arm to hold my finger with his tiny hand.

We gave him the middle name Macauley.

Dear little guy,

The day before you were born, I superglued my eyes shut. (How I did it is a story for another time.) The eye doctor flushed the glue out of my eyes, and now I can see.

Now that you've been in my life for four years, I feel like my eyes were glued shut my whole life before you. You've opened up a whole new part of me I didn't know existed. Thank you for making me a dad.

We gave you the middle name Macauley, so no matter where you go, your first neighbourhood will always be a part of you. It's the roughest neighbourhood in the city, but you love exploring it. You love going to Lucky 97 for mango candies, the Italian Centre for gelato, Giovanni Caboto Park for the slides and swings. I cherish our McCauley adventures.

Your birth had some rough parts, but it all led to you being here. And I love every bit of you, especially the rough parts. Nothing in this whole world could ever make me stop loving you.

Dada

# The Day We Were Born

**By Ryan Lacanilao**

When you were born,
our doula said it was strange:
Only your head was sticking out,
and you opened your eyes to look around.

For the past nine months,
your world was darkness,
warmth, heartbeats, and muffled voices—
an astronaut floating in liquid space.

Did you hear Netflix?
*Tiger King, Love is Blind,*
Every season of *Master Chef.*
We stayed home; you quarantined in the womb.

Then you were born,
head sticking out, silent.
I didn't know you couldn't breathe.
They pushed a tube down your throat, then you cried.

Stunned by the cold,
a different kind of light
and by the need to use your lungs,
and to be fed, to be held, to be loved.

The day you were born,
I stuck my head out, silent—
stunned by the new world you pulled me into.

As you slept on my chest
all wrapped up, but you freed an arm
so your tiny hand could hold my finger.

Your little snore,
squeaks, opening one eye—
a knowing wink, like you could tell
I was discovering this for the first time too.

And as we grow,
I'll always remember
we took our first breath together,
because the day you were born so was I.

# A Distant Homeland

## By Marvin Cao

FROM THE WINDOW OF HIS 27TH-FLOOR APARTMENT, KAI GAZED OUT AT a typical winter scene in Edmonton, Canada. The trees along the street stood bare, their dark, twisted branches exposed. The road stretched far into the distance, and as Kai stared at the distant skyline, he could almost see his old home in Beijing and a busy, ordinary life in a traditional courtyard house not so long ago...

## The Call to Leave

The courtyard house, or "siheyuan," is a traditional housing form commonly found in Beijing and northern China. It consists of four low buildings surrounding a central courtyard, with each building serving a different function. This architectural style has reportedly existed for over 2,500 years. Due to Beijing's urban redevelopment, these large land homes became increasingly rare in the city after 2010, replaced by more modern, high-rise buildings that made more efficient use of land. The remaining courtyard houses were either converted into tourist attractions or transformed into luxurious residences for the wealthy, complete with modern amenities and price tags ranging from six to over one hundred million Canadian dollars.

Kai considered himself fortunate to have lived in one of these traditional courtyard houses, with its authentic charm. Kai, his wife Bei, and his parents lived in opposite wings of the house. To access shared spaces like the living room or bathroom, they had to cross the open courtyard. While this traditional layout might seem at odds with modern living, it reflected the Chinese ideals of harmony with nature.

Kai's courtyard house was in Fangshan, a distant suburb of Beijing. This meant that on every workday, he had to leave home by 7 a.m. to drive to the nearest subway station. There, he would join thousands of others cramming onto the Fangshan Line. Despite trains arriving every minute, Kai had to fight his way onto the nearest one, as waiting never reduced the chance of being pushed off at the next stop. This process repeated at least three more times each morning, as he transferred from the Fangshan Line to Lines 9, 4, and 10. If everything went smoothly, he would arrive at his office by 9 a.m. The evening commute was equally grueling, often bringing him home after 9 p.m. This meant Kai spent every workday of the year returning under the stars.

Bei's job was located in Haidian District and required a similar commute, though her work hours were more flexible. According to China's population statistics, Beijing's permanent population was 21.886 million in 2021, more than half of Canada's total population. The population density was equivalent to squeezing all of Canadians into Vancouver Island.

Kai and Bei were both tied down by this demanding work-life rhythm, but at least it provided them with a stable, middle-class income. It also allowed them to travel, for example, in 2018 when they went to Florence, Italy for their honeymoon, Kai's first trip abroad. Unlike most Chinese travelers who choose Southeast Asia for their first international trip, Kai and Bei ventured to distant Europe—a decision made by Bei.

"It's hard to imagine this scene on an ordinary workday after getting off work," Kai said, as he eyed groups of men and women sitting leisurely by the fountain in a small square, colorful blankets beneath them, chatting over beers. The setting sun bathed the spire and stone walls of an ancient church in golden light. "It was as if the world's worries and busyness didn't exist." This ordinary day in a small town outside Florence etched itself into Kai's memory, leaving a deep impression. It gave him a glimpse of how slower life could be. Then, two subsequent events made him seriously consider the option of leaving Beijing.

In 2020, Kai and Bei spent the Chinese New Year in the UK. In Edinburgh, Scotland, they touched the bronze statue of David Hume, who represented the pinnacle of British empiricism. Legend has it that touching the statue brings wisdom, and the polished bronze of Hume's right big toe attested to its popularity. For Kai and Bei, it was also a blessing for the new life growing inside Bei.

Edinburgh was the final stop of their UK trip, but a shadow loomed over their hearts. News of a rapidly spreading virus began to circulate, the Chinese city of Wuhan had been completely locked down. Fear and uncertainty about the virus fueled rumors of European countries closing their borders, leaving international travelers anxious.

The pandemic posed many restrictions all over China. The government used different means to track individuals' movements, marking areas and times visited by infected people to assess personal risk levels and prevent contamination. There were three levels: green for normal, red for mandatory quarantine in centralized facilities, and yellow for home isolation. During the third year of the pandemic, and a business trip to a neighboring city Kai was marked as yellow and considered a potential risk by the authorities. He had to be strictly isolated from his family.

Community workers locked him in his wing of the courtyard house, forcing Bei to move out. He had to prove that he could manage all his "needs" within the room, except for food, which was delivered regularly.

The bathroom, however, was in another part of the courtyard, requiring him to cross the open yard. As a result, Kai was forced to use a makeshift toilet that Bei had used during her pregnancy, placed in the room as a solution. But he still vividly remembers the lowered voices and cautious demeanor of the community workers as they left. "We'll lock the door, but the window will stay open."

"At the worst point, I had to climb out the window just to use a proper washroom." Kai explained

During those times when he had to climb out the window, Kai often recalled the beautiful moments from his travels, like that ordinary day in the Italian town. Even though those trips had happened not long ago, the sense of leisure and joy was a distant memory.

The birth of their son, DuDu, was the second reason for choosing to leave. DuDu was born in 2020, shortly after Kai and Bei returned from the UK, meaning he entered the world during the pandemic. This brought additional challenges to his early life, as limited medical resources were stretched even thinner. But it also gave the young couple more time to reflect on their son's growth and future.

"My wish was simple: I hope DuDu has a healthy and happy childhood, where he can retain the natural curiosity and play-fulness of a child," Kai said. In some ways, Chinese children have it much harder than their parents. Traditional Chinese emphasis on education and the desire for children to succeed often leads to early exposure to rigorous academic training. This is seen as an act of love, as success in life requires "winning at the starting line." This mindset is so pervasive that even parents who believe in a more relaxed approach to education find it hard to escape.

Kai and Bei made a firm decision to leave this restrictive environment around mid-2022. Once the decision was made, the young couple moved with remarkable speed.

## The Journey

*1. Adopt a proactive learning attitude; don't rely on external environments to change you.*

*2. Be active in class. Sit in the front and sit with local classmates. Don't worry about awkwardness...*

*3. Engage with the teacher during class—answer questions or ask your own. Sitting in the front gives you an advantage because the teacher can hear you clearly and may even give feedback...*

*4. Use breaks to chat with classmates. Between classes, while waiting for the next teacher to arrive, everyone gathers in the hallway to chat. Join in, even if you're just listening...*

*5. Join student clubs or activities to meet new people and expand your social circle. During activities or games, you'll naturally pick up new words and phrases, and because they're used in real-life contexts, you'll remember them better.*

*6. Consider living in university housing. Most dorms are shared, and you can choose roommates based on lifestyle preferences. Living with international roommates is a great way to practice English daily and learn about their culture and habits...*

*7. Make time to study English daily, even outside of class. Be proactive — take lessons with a tutor, watch American TV shows, or use English dictionaries to understand new words...*

This is a memorandum of Kai's English learning experience during his first semester at NAIT, shared on Red Note, "xiaohongshu" in Chinese, a Chinese social media platform. At 35, an age often associated with career crises in China and the cutoff for civil service exams, Kai found himself starting over in a foreign country after 12 years away from school. His post resonated with many strangers, sparking enthusiastic responses.

His destination was not the sunny hills of Tuscany but Edmonton, with its long, harsh winters. Upon arriving in Canada, Kai faced numerous challenges, starting with the language barrier. For Kai and his generation, formal English education began early, typically in fifth grade. English was a core subject, heavily weighted in exams for middle school, university, and even some civil service positions. A university degree often requires proof of English proficiency. However, for most Chinese, English was merely a tool for exams, not a practical skill. According to EF EPI 2023, the English proficiency of Chinese people ranks 82nd in the world. China's ancestors are famous for building the Great Wall, but the language barrier is an even more abstract and far-reaching divide. As the only widely used and still-evolving pictographic language, square Chinese characters are like bricks in this linguistic Great Wall.

After 12 years away from university, Kai had to transform English from an exam tool into a practical skill. "Back then, I studied until at least 1 a.m. every night." He listened to English programs while driving, memorized vocabulary on the subway, and stayed late at the office to study—his manager, who thought he was working overtime for free, was happy.

Kai thought he understood the Western world. His life in China had fueled his curiosity about Western society, from its political systems to its culture. Aristotle, John Locke, and Hayek were among his favorite and influential authors. Yet, upon arriving in Canada, he found himself struggling with mundane and menial tasks: taking the bus (not knowing to pull the cord or press a button to signal his stop), crossing the street (some intersections require pressing a button to activate the signal), eating fast food (not realizing you're supposed to clean your tray), shopping (some stores require membership cards and don't provide bags), and socializing (struggling to remember classmates' names or subway station names).

Before Halloween, their programming teacher said they could either dress up for the next class or submit their homework on Monday. Kai was the only one who chose the latter—and the only one who didn't wear a costume. He was also the only Chinese student in his class, who paid four times the tuition of locals.

Kai was continuously feeling out of place. The mismatched furniture in his new apartment added a touch of absurdity to the scene. Yet, these struggles paled in comparison to the pain of being separated from his family. Before leaving China, Bei's work visa was denied again, forcing the couple to live on opposite sides of the globe. Bei remained in their Beijing courtyard house with Kai's parents, raising their son in a typical Chinese family arrangement.

"You can't understand what it feels like," Kai said calmly over the phone, though the emotion in his voice was palpable. Missing this stage of being with his growing son was unbearable, and Kai found solace only in video calls across the Pacific. DuDu, still young, gazed curiously at the screen, unsure why his father's image and voice came from a phone. He might not yet understand the meaning of "Dad," but for Kai, each call was a lifeline, a pillar supporting his life and studies in Edmonton.

## Where Lies Home?

In the spring of 2024, Bei finally arrived in Canada with DuDu, reuniting the family of three. It was a moment of joy and relief, a fragile victory in their long journey. Bei had entered as a tourist—a stroke of luck, given the high risks associated with her visa application after her work visa was denied. But this also meant she had no legal right to work, at least for the time being. The family's sole income was now their savings, stretched thin by the soaring costs of rent, a car, and raising a child.

They rarely shopped at T&T, a popular Asian supermarket chain, because it was too expensive. Instead, they scoured different stores for discounted items, playing a game of "retail guerrilla warfare" to stretch their budget. Their 27th-floor apartment became DuDu's playground. Beyond that, the apartment was sparsely furnished—not even a pair of matching chairs, reflecting their financial constraints, a life pared down to the bare essentials.

Kai was studying Electronic Engineering at NAIT, a stark departure from his business degree in China. This shift meant abandoning over a decade of professional experience, while Kai insisted his decision wasn't solely about practicality.

Then in October 2024, electronic engineering was removed from NAIT's list of programs eligible for post-graduation work permits. This meant future international students in the program would no longer have a direct path to immigration. While Kai's status was unaffected for now, the ever-shifting immigration policies and tightening restrictions added a layer of anxiety to their lives. What was once considered a reliable path to permanent residency was now fraught with uncertainty.

The 2024 Christmas holiday offered little respite for Kai and Bei. DuDu fell ill, and Kai had to dedicate time to prepare for an English proficiency test—a new requirement for his work permit application. This hurdle, which had not existed just months earlier, was another sign of the narrowing immigration pathway.

Despite the challenges, Kai remained optimistic. He attended every class diligently, sought out internship opportunities, and dreamed of the future. Kai dreamt of taking his family to Banff once he gets his work permit. He dreamt of buying an RV and travelling once they have their permanent residency. These dreams kept him hopeful. Yet, his words also hinted at a bittersweet reality. If their trip to Europe years ago had been a luxury of time and distance, even a short trip now felt like a luxury of the spirit.

The pandemic, with its absurdities and hardships, had faded into the background, almost as if it had never happened. Kai harbored no resentment, though. In fact, he was content with their new life. Compared to the hustle of Beijing, Edmonton offered clear advantages, especially for raising a child. "When you have a child, you start evaluating life through their eyes," he said. "This is a better environment for DuDu to explore, play, and stay innocent."

"We didn't move abroad for economic reasons," Kai emphasized repeatedly when discussing the financial impact of their decision. For many middle-class Chinese immigrant families, this might be true. But Kai's insistence seemed to carry an unspoken subtext. Sometimes, we live within the narratives we construct for ourselves, constantly justifying our choices to others, and to ourselves.

The Chinese diaspora is perhaps one of the most rooted and tradition-bound communities in the world. In Edmonton, I noticed traces of this everywhere—older immigrants dressed and behaved as they had before they left China decades ago. The city's name, Edmonton, even had at least four different Chinese translation: "埃德蒙顿" in simplified Chinese in Mainland China, "愛德蒙頓" in Traditional Chinese in Taiwan, "愛民頓" in Cantonese, and "點問頓" in Taishan dialect. Each reflecting the cultural and regional diversity of its Chinese community. In a way, Edmonton was a mosaic of different eras and regions of China, each group interpreting their choices and their distant homeland in their own way.

I once asked DuDu whether he preferred life in Beijing or Edmonton. He responded with the blank, innocent gaze of a child. "He doesn't have that concept yet," Bei said with a smile. "To him, Beijing and Edmonton are just two different places to play." In that moment, I felt a pang of shame for imposing my adult complexities on his childlike simplicity.

But the question lingered: In this vast world, where lies the ideal home? From the 27th-floor apartment, the answer drifts in the winter night, elusive yet ever-present.

Raymond Keung, "Alberta Legislature Building" Watercolour 2023

# Finding My Way Home

**By Cynthia Palmaria**

"BUT WHY ARE YOU MOVING TO DEADMONTON?" OUR FRIENDS IN Toronto teased us non-stop as we said goodbye.

"We will be leaving our 'family' and we know no one in Edmonton," my 12-year-old daughter exclaimed.

She was referring to a handful of *titas* (aunties) and cousins among the community members in Toronto who she has come to love. I masked my sadness and quickly reassured her, "Don't worry honey, we will build a new 'family' there.' I was apprehensive to leave Toronto's busy life yet excited for what our new life has to offer.

The decision to move our family to Edmonton came after I grabbed the opportunity to teach in the healthcare field in one of the universities there. Teaching is a passion that I discovered while I was a young health science student in Quebec and started tutoring for extra money. After I graduated, I worked in the healthcare field and a few years later, a door opened for a teaching profession. This shift in my career allowed my family to experience several Canadian provinces. In Toronto, we were in our third province and if you are wondering why keep moving, it was the quest for a better and balanced life, less driving (which Toronto could not offer), and the chance to continue organizing with the community.

In the different cities where we previously lived, my husband and I were strongly connected with our *kababayans*, our fellow Filipinos. A lot of them were new migrants, especially those who needed support and found a family in our community. Wherever we were, we found a way to share our migration stories, discuss how our society forced families to be separated, and organize ourselves for change. We worked through our challenges and fought for the most vulnerable workers while we all aspired for a better future, here and back home in the Philippines. My husband and I were certain that we wanted to continue our activism once we moved to Edmonton. I was thrilled yet also nervous as I looked forward to our new life, my teaching career, a dynamic community to connect with, and of course, many new adventures.

Making plans to move was not an easy task especially when I realized that, due to work, I had to move earlier by myself. I left Toronto while my family stayed behind to pack our old life in boxes and get ready for a new beginning. We reached out to the only friend we had in Edmonton who was a fellow Montrealer from our activist circle. Fortunately, she was willing to guide and support my transition, especially in finding my way around a strange city as I searched for housing. Knowing that I had a supportive friend who was also very much connected to the community mattered a lot. I preoccupied myself with work and at the end of the day, I felt lonely without my family. I felt devoid of human contact after work unless I forced myself to socialize with my housemates who were strangers. I was away from my husband and daughter for four months. During this time, I could truly relate to the migrant stories of separation, parenting and family dinner conversations only through video calls.

This experience felt like the stories of community members who were continents apart from their loved ones. It was during those four months that I felt the heartbreak of family separation, stories that are too common in my community where parents are forced to be away from their children. My parents' narrative was no different from other Filipino migrant workers, who left their home country to work abroad for a better future for the whole family.

Being uprooted from home to an unfamiliar country, a new city, to be among different people was something I experienced as a teenager. When my sister and I migrated to Canada to join our parents, I remember feeling mixed emotions of excitement, sadness, and nervousness in anticipation of new adventures. Moving from Toronto to Edmonton conjured similar emotions in me but this time, I was in some ways more prepared and strengthened with the knowledge of my own parents' and other migrants' stories of courage.

My new-found friends in the community became my support system in Edmonton. Friends and families readily welcomed me into their homes where we celebrated events together, shared meals, and I even got the chance to read books to their children. I met many new people and attended weddings, birthday parties, and picnics where I learned more about our community's concerns. The feeling of loneliness slowly transformed into the joy of feeling that I belonged, where home cooked meals nourished me, migrant stories enlightened me, and overcoming struggles inspired me.

Those four months of separation felt long for me, but it was incomparable to many years or even decades of family separation experienced by most migrants. As a community activist, our hope is for migrant families to be reunited or better yet, for families to lead a decent life together in our homeland.

Just months after my family joined me in Edmonton, we found a new home of our own and became more entrenched in community work. It is the community, our new family, which warms my heart in the -40C winters in Edmonton. As I promised our daughter, we built a new 'home and family' in Edmonton as we continued to advocate for and with the migrants in their struggle for a better life here and back home.

Somehow, I still long for the day when I will wake up to the cock's crow, feel the warmth of the tropical sun on my skin, and enjoy the view of the lush mountains outside my window, which was my life before moving to another country. In the meantime, home is always where the community is and right now, it is Edmonton.

**Ulrike Rossier, "Self-Portrait"**

Born in West Germany in the midst of World War II, Ulrike (Uli) Rossier
came to Canada to raise her family. In 2021, Uli was chosen as the Nina's
Artist of the Year. See more of her art here:

WWW.THENINA.CA/ARTISTS/ULRIKE-ROSSIER/

# The Art of Uli

**By Oliver Rossier**

## 1980 - Wolf Creek, Alberta, Canada

LATE WINTER, EARLY SPRING. THE BRIGHT GLOWING GREEN OF NEW leaves is starting to shimmer in the poplar and aspen forest beside the road. The sheep bunch up near the drier parts of the pasture, nibbling away at the early grasses.

There could be black bears, or coyotes, but the dogs would smell them and be barking if they were this close to the house.

I pick up rocks from the gravel road and toss them hard at the gnarly black parts of trees. Whenever I bend down, I smell the wet vibrant earth. That does not improve my mood.

I whip another rock at another tree. Throw, miss again.

"Oliver, hurry up, supper's ready!" I hear my sister Caroline call.

So what? I throw another rock, miss another tree.

The sun is almost setting, but I could still see the dark brown of the cedar sided house, the grey of the cement basement, and the pale face of Caroline waving emphatically at me from the balcony. She waves at me the same way she waves at the sheep when we need to move the stupid animals from one area to another.

"What's the big deal? Why can't I just eat at Darren's?" I shouted.

"Dad wants to talk, he brought some pizza from Edson."

Well, that's a big improvement over the 'stone soup' we often eat these days. Dad is a horrible cook and often tried to put everything into a pot and throw in a few spices. Mom had been a much better cook, but nothing is normal anymore.

—

Mom was found on a dirt road by one of the neighbours. Rushing to the Edson hospital ended up wasting precious time. The Edson hospital sent her to the University Hospital in Edmonton after futile hours trying to sort out why a very healthy 35-year-old would collapse into a coma.

Everything changed with the aneurysm. I went from being surrounded by layers of love, to being surrounded by layers of need. At the time, it felt like my heart was ripped out of my body. There was just a gaping hole of uncertainty in the centre of my world. Breathing seemed harder. Bright sunny days did not make any sense, why should there be warmth when everything inside me is frozen.

When my Mom finally woke from a coma after eight weeks, she had lost significant parts of her memory, and vision in one eye. She looked vaguely at us for months, not really recognizing us. That got a bit better when Dad took her out of the hospital – six months after the aneurysm and against doctors' advice – and moved her back to our farm in Wolf Creek.

Unfortunately, Mom also came out with a rupture in her esophagus and windpipe; so she had to be fed by a tube into her stomach. And the tube kept popping out.

---

"Dad, help!" Nina is inside, but she could yell.

"What?"

"The tube popped out again!"

I heard the fast rumble of Dad's feet pounding on the stairs inside the house. I ran up the balcony stairs. In moments, Caroline and I hover in the doorway of our parents' bedroom. We watched as Dad grabbed a wire coat hanger and slipped it carefully in the gastro-tube that feeds Mom. My eldest sister, Nina, kept her hand on the gauze pads pressed up against Mom's stomach so that no more of the acidic stomach fluid could ooze out and add to the pink flesh already swelling around the tube.

"Ok, get ready!" Dad was steady, moving the tube over Mom's stomach.

"Now." He moved Nina's hand and the gauze aside and slid the tube back in.

Mom winced a bit but then opened her eyes wide and looked at us. "Oh, Arturo, I'm so sorry to make you worry so much." Her face was still scarred and malformed since all the operations on her skull, but her eyes and voice still held oceans of love.

Dad carefully wiped her stomach. "What are you talking about Uli, you didn't do that on purpose. Let's just get you cleaned up and then we can eat, too." It's amazing how gentle he was with her.

"I'm on a strict diet, do you know what 'DIET' stands for?" Mom was always trying to make us smile, even if she quickly forgets that she has just told us the same joke. "Did I Eat That - DIET..." She looked up to the roomful of smiles she expected.

The emergency was handled, we filed out to wash our hands and to dig into the pizza.

—

"We're moving to Edmonton. This summer." Dad announced. "I'm going to study psychology."

Dad is all wiry strength, most of that strength seemed to come from anger. Anger at being raised in an abusive orphanage in Switzerland, anger at institutions, anger at a world that would take his life partner away and give him another dependent.

There was a tense pause at the table, then the questions tumbled out.

"What, and leave all the animals?" Nina loved her horse. She also loved to throw daggers at Dad. "And how are you going to study Psychology when you haven't even finished high school?"

"What are we going to do there, where will we go to school?" Gina asked.

"Why don't you just get your job back with CN so that we can stay here?" I muttered. Caroline stayed quiet, big brown eyes watching everything.

Dad glowered and did not bother to answer any of our questions. "We can't stay here anymore, I'm sick of it! And if I got back to CN - who would take care of Uli? You guys cannot even do the chores without arguing all the time. I'm sick of it! I can't do this anymore!" Dad's hand exploded on the table and his chair crashed against the wall.

The conversation was over. The decision was made.

The kids sat in quiet tension until we heard the door slam downstairs. Caroline started crying.

"This is your fault, Oliver, you're always arguing when we have to divide the chores." Nina was always good at delegating blame.

"Eat cow pies, Nina." I retorted and went upstairs to my dusty but immense attic room. I had the whole top floor to myself. Except for the seedlings Dad experimented with. Dad was always experimenting, almost frantically, trying to find any way of helping Mom get back to normal. Miracle cures were welcome, hope was the lifeline.

It was fun to watch some of the expensive crystals he hung in windows. They spun rainbows around the room when the sun pierced them. And it was pretty funny that Dad bought a small glass pyramid and tried to grow avocados from an avocado pit... in Alberta... in winter...

I looked at the strangled little branch that peeked out of the avocado pit. There was actually one shiny green leaf, but the whole pyramid smelled more like mold than avocado.

The leaf would die, and fall away, just like our life on the farm.

—

**September 2009 - Edmonton, Alberta, Canada**

It was a warm evening, fall winds were blowing yellow leaves around the crowd gathered on 118 Ave in Edmonton. People were gathered around a new building, about to open.

Farther up the street, I squeezed a rusty white Ford Escape into a parking spot.

"Here we are, an hour and a half late… thanks Nina, we almost missed the whole thing." I grumbled as Dad jumped out of his seat to help Mom get her seat buckle undone.

The speeches had started under the clear dark sky as we finally got moving toward the ceremony.

"Thank you for coming to help us celebrate the official opening of the Nina Haggerty Centre!" The event MC was a writer for the Edmonton Journal, and several national and international magazines. He was also the President of the Nina Haggerty Centre board, and he knew how to mobilize people. "The Mayor is here and he'd like to say a few words."

"Thank you! Ladies and gentlemen, it is a great honour for my wife and I to be here with you today to celebrate this wonderful occasion. The Nina Haggerty Centre staff and board deserve a big round of applause for all their work." The Mayor had the crowd in his hands, and his wife was glowing, surrounded by friends, and cheering fans.

Our family clapped along with the rest of the crowd. Mom did her happy dance, bounced her head up and down while her eyes moved in slightly different directions. We were all smiling.

I stepped back and scanned the scene. Compulsively counting, I estimated about 50 people gathered loosely along 118 Ave, and there were also quite a few people inside the building already. The glass windows of the Nina Haggerty Centre gave a good view of the long tables where the artists worked. I could also see food and drinks being handed out, reminding me that I had not eaten yet.

"Hey, Oliver, great that you guys could make it! We're always so glad to see Uli!" Wendy Hollo, the Executive Director, was a bundle of energy. She gripped my shoulder and smiled warmly at me before giving a big hug to Mom and the rest of the family.

"We're here to celebrate the Nina Haggerty Centre. This is a space for artists of a wide range of abilities to find themselves and build themselves as artists. Develop and nurture their capacities in a safe space." The MC paused.

"We're also here to raise funds for the Nina... and I've just thought of a new opportunity." He paused for dramatic effect and pointed at the new sign on the side of the building. "What if we take this opportunity to auction off all the letters of the Nina Haggerty Centre name?"

"What, we just put them up!" Wendy shouted. Everyone laughed.

"How about we start with $500 each letter and help this amazing centre get more art supplies?" The MC swept his smiling eyes across the crowd, welcoming bids.

Nina's arm shot up, "We'll buy 4 letters: N - I - N - A !"

"Wow, Nina! Did you win the lottery?" Wendy poked Nina in the side, surprised, But I am used to all this. We are a gypsy clan, with big hearts, and empty bank accounts, but somehow we always manage to make it work. Especially to help Mom make art.

Wendy put her hand on my shoulder and lowered her voice. "Actually, Oliver, I wanted to talk to you about the exhibit we have planned for your Mom. She had been with us since we started the program at the old location on 111 Ave! And everyone loves her artwork, such beautiful designs and bright colours. We are trying to figure out what to call the exhibit. Do you want to talk it over as a family, and send us a few ideas?"

"Sure, I will do that."

"Sold! Thank you everyone!" The MC sold all the letters of the new sign. "Come on into this beautiful space that you helped create!"

We cheered and went into the building. Nina and Dad got tangled up trying to pull Mom through different sides of the same door.

"Hey, I'm not a puppet... I don't have any strings." Mom squinted at the artwork hanging near the door. "I'm blind in one eye. Let's see what I can see. Look at all that green, my favourite colour. Oh, that's my painting!" She pointed. The very distinct style of abstract painting, filling the canvas with bright colours, triangles, squares and circles intricately woven together was definitely Mom's unique style

"And there's already a red dot on it, so it's sold!"

"But I'm not so old," rhymed my Mom. "I helped raise eight children, birthed three, I like to be with children, the more the merrier. Kind of makes sense, I'm the sixth of ten children myself. And here's my big baby…he was born smiling…"

"How could I do anything else… you were always smiling back at me." I looked at her and her beautiful paintings and thought about her healing journey. It all felt like a miracle.

———

*My Mom was a force of nature. Mom was a tireless caregiver, a wiry tough tree planter, a gardener, a farmer and a parent. Mother of three birth children, she also raised five other children at various stages. She and my Dad took in any nephews or nieces when her brothers and sisters were struggling.*

*Art was always a part of Mom's life. She helped set up the first craft centre in Edson. She worked with her friends Anne Steffes and Wendy Andrews to organize weaving, pottery, and painting classes.*

*Art was also a big part of my Mom's healing. For many years after we first moved to Edmonton, Mom bounced around between various programs. No one seemed to know what to do for her. For a few years, the Northern Alberta Brain Injury Service, known as NABIS, seemed*

*to be doing good things with people with diverse health issues. But NABIS got shut down during the budget cuts in the Ralph Klein years.*

*We kept looking and trying different programs. Then we stumbled onto the SKILLS programs just as they were setting up the Nina Haggerty Centre, and what a blessing that was.*

—

I looked around the gallery. There was a procession of other artists coming up to chat with Mom, who was beaming in front of a whole wall covered with her paintings. Dad was beside her, holding her hand.

"Uli, look at the church I made!" One of the artists rolled up in her wheelchair, holding a multi-coloured pottery. "Look at the roof, it has my thumbprints."

"Oh, that's very pretty. You might put a little more green on the roof. Did you know green is the colour of life? I used to do pottery too, and I used to go to church." Mom said with a glint in her eye, warming up to a familiar story. "I would go to confession and tell the priest a whole set of stories. And then, at the very end… I would tell him that I lied."

Everyone laughed.

Mom started eating but continued talking. "I'm pretty sure I can eat that. I'm on a diet, do you know what diet stands for…"

The artist had heard Mom's diet joke before. She turned to Dad and asked if he liked it.

"I like your art, but I don't like churches." Dad answers flatly.

"Why? Did you know that Edmonton is in the Guiness Book of world records for the most churches in the smallest area? Why don't you like churches?"

"When I was a kid, I was raised in an orphanage run by a church in Switzerland… They sold me like a slave."

I moved over to stand by Dad, put my hand on his shoulder.

There's a brief pause, then the artist tried a different question. "What do you do now? For work?"

Dad took a breath and reset himself. "Well, I worked on the railways, and then I studied nursing, and then I worked in a hardware store. But really, I'm a nurse." He was still holding Mom's hand, watching her, ready with a napkin to catch anything that stays on her chin.

Wendy, beside me again, signaled to the musicians to start their next set. She guided me over to the food. "Your Dad has had an amazing life. How long did he do all those different jobs?"

"Well, he worked with the CN railway, in Jasper and Edson, for about 12 years. Then he came to Edmonton and studied psychology and nursing, worked as a nurse up North in Fort Simpson, and then Montreal, for a total of about 12 years. But he had really been a nurse ever since my Mom's aneurysm."

I said this while looking at my parents and came up with an idea. "And actually… we have a name for the exhibit."

I pointed at my parents. "The Nina has given our Mom such a great place to find community and meaning, despite all her health challenges. She's really thrived here. When people ask her what she does, she always says she's an artist. But there's no way she could have done that without devoted support… from the Nina… from my Dad. The exhibit name would have a double meaning, her art that she paints, and her Arturo… Art. The exhibit name? The Art of Uli."

Ulrike Rossier, "Yesterday-Today"

# *meaningful* connections

"We are each other's harvest, we are each other's business; we are each other's magnitude and bond." – Gwendolyn Brooks

# It's A Small World

**By Jesus Tigulo**

I AM FROM THE GLOBAL SOUTH, NOW LIVING IN THE GLOBAL NORTH. To me, these are merely two sides of the same coin.

Over a decade ago, I left the Philippines together with my family as immigrants, to go to a place foreign to us then - the great white land mass called Canada. The Canada that I knew as a young boy, I learned it all from a school library: reading magazines, books, and specially the encyclopedia where nations' origins, histories, cultures, and values are described, then visualized through images of people, pictures of land masses, and beautiful sceneries. What I imagined about Canada was limited to that information alone, and I had no idea what awaited in real life.

In 2010, it was nighttime when we arrived in Vancouver, British Columbia. At the airport lobby, we saw a huge banner for "2010 Winter Olympics," and we learned then that this province just hosted a major Winter Olympics sporting event.

We passed through immigration control without much ado. At this point, my wife called our contact persons in Edmonton to inform them of our anticipated arrival time. After a short layover, our journey continued, and we arrived past midnight in Edmonton.

"It's very cold, Papa." Those were the first four words my eldest child uttered. In silence, I also felt the piercing coldness of the night. My two other daughters innocently chorused: "We feel the same way, Papa." Their mother signaled to come closer and huddle together to keep warm.

My children were filled with curiosity. I myself was surprised, seeing the outdoor scenes: snow packed along the roadside, cars covered with dirt, people with muddied shoes, jackets, scarves, gloves, toques – people's entire bodies were covered. Little did I know then that harsh winter will visit us every year in this place where we have now chosen to live for the rest of our lives.

Very exhausted and feeling drowsy, my mind raced back to the time when we decided to leave our homeland to seek greener pastures elsewhere. While in the middle of thinking about the Canadian dream, along the highway towards the city proper, I saw a wooden marker 'Welcome to the City of Edmonton-Alberta's capital city." Just below this line, a phrase caught my eye: City of Champions.

I knew nothing about that phrase then. I thought, perhaps it was just some kind of a catch phrase or an important event worth re-membering, but I had no clue what. As a new immigrant, it was not my foremost concern. My focus in my adopted home was to work, build a life for the betterment of my family, nothing more. Looking back, should I say I was selfish? In a sense, maybe, but at the back of my mind, I think many immigrants also have the same aspirations and ideas.

In 2015, that slogan was no longer in the wooden marker, and I wondered why. My mind raced back, trying to recollect what was the significance of these three little words. But still, my mind would always shift to: Why should I care? But the slogan did not leave my mind altogether.

One day, I was inside a bus shelter waiting for my ride home, surrounded by the sound of drizzling rain pattering over the roof. I was alone when minutes later, a shadowy person came towards me. He stepped inside, wearing a toque that almost fully covered his bushy face.

"Got a smoke my friend?" he asked.

"Nope," I uttered.

I saw him looking at my hand holding a coffee cup, and the shiny watch and golden bracelet in my left wrist. He moved a little bit closer to me, with his right hand inside his coat. At this point, I was getting a little bit nervous.

"How about your coffee, could you spare it? It is cold, I need to warm up."

My instinct said fight or flight, but this guy asked me politely. So, I decided to invite him.

"Hey, there's a coffee shop across the street, would you like to go there and have coffee, chat, and we can take our time?" I asked. He agreed, and off we went together.

Inside was packed with people, and I could smell the freshness of freshly brewed coffee. In one corner, we noticed three men and two empty chairs. Suddenly, one guy motioned us to come over.

"Oh! I know them," the guy with me said. We went to them, and he said, "Good to see you all brothers."

I ended up talking with the group for some time, covering a lot of topics: politics, human interest, social issues. I enjoyed talking to them, though we did not introduce ourselves. These nameless people seemed very knowledgeable to me, and their appearance showed they are of various heritages.

During our conversation, I asked if anyone knew why Edmonton was called City of Champions. The guy sitting opposite me, with an Oilers jersey and fez hat covering his forehead, pointed his fingers towards his chest.

"We were many times NHL hockey champions, and we all stand up proud of the achievement of our players at that time."

Another guy with a beret hat butted in. "Also, because a tornado struck our city back in 1987 and residents showed up to help the victims and clean up the debris left by that natural disaster."

So, I learned of those two momentous events when people of different colours and backgrounds came together as one community in times of sadness and happiness. Because of that, our city officials adopted the slogan Edmonton City of Champions as a tribute to the unsung heroes.

"But is it not ironic that we celebrate both sadness and happiness in one slogan?" I interrupted.

Everyone was a bit surprised, and a lull in the conversation followed.

Breaking the silence, I asked, "Why was the slogan removed?"

My new friend spoke slowly, bending his head towards me, he said "Edmonton was not the first city to coin that phrase. So, do we want to be called a copycat? Besides, it is not all encompassing. For example, why celebrate sports accomplishments alone? Why not create a slogan that defines Edmonton as Edmonton! Rich in arts and culture, vibrant, diverse, a city of festivals and a city we can all call uniquely ours."

The guy with a baseball cap, joined the fray. "Is it not a good idea that a slogan of a city should be part of its heritage, and it should be an evolving and generational tagline?"

"It should be a tagline that shows the world that Edmonton people can do extraordinary things when duty calls," another added.

Another pause in the conversation ensued. I looked at my watch, although I was actually wearing a dead watch, "Time to go home for me," I said.

Two of us left first, and the three guys we met inside the coffeeshop stayed behind. They remained nameless to me, but I did not want it to be that way with the first person I met at the bus stop who enriched my experience in this new city that night.

Before we parted ways, I introduced myself: "My name is Jesus. What's your name?"

"My name is Mohammed," he said, smiling.

I smiled too.

Two no-longer-strangers, with different values and cultures, living in a city we now call home.

Randy Stennes, "Coffee-Tea"

# My Growth and Transformation with Natasha

**By Yanjian Luo**

### A Ray of Hope in a New Land

My wife Julie and I both looked out of the airplane window, taking one last look at the towering skyline of Shanghai. The familiar city lights gradually faded into the distance. Our hearts filled with a mix of hesitancy and anticipation. We embarked on a journey to Canada under our beloved son's sponsorship, knowing we were stepping into an unfamiliar world.

On March 10, 2024, we arrived in Edmonton known as the "Gateway to the North." The sky was clear, with sunlight casting its glow over the frozen ground. Yet, the March air was crisp and chilly, starkly different from the warmth and humidity of Shanghai. We stepped out of the airport into the lingering coolness of winter, our first introduction to the city's atmosphere — both foreign and fascinating. This was the beginning of a new chapter in our lives.

For me, the challenges went beyond adjusting to the climate and time differences; language and cultural barriers presented even greater obstacles. Life moved at an unfamiliar and slower pace, my daily routines were filled with uncertainties, making every step feel like a test.

Back in China, I had been a senior metro design engineer, and Julie had worked as a chief physician at a major hospital. However, in this foreign land, our professional identities seemed to dissolve, leaving us feeling like beginners again. The fluent conversations we once had now felt hesitant and fragmented. Everything had to start from scratch. Many barriers had to be overcome.

## A Path to Learning: Finding Hope in the Library

To adapt to this new life, language was the first barrier we needed to overcome. I began attending English conversation circles at the Edmonton Public Library. There, I met a group of kind-hearted volunteers, many of whom were former educators dedicated to helping newcomers integrate into Canadian society. Among them was Shelagh, an elegant and stylish woman who had previously taught at the LINC (Language Instruction for Newcomers to Canada) program. Understanding the language struggles of immigrants, Shelagh spoke slowly and gently corrected pronunciations, encouraging learners to express themselves confidently.

I was drawn to her lessons — not just because of her patience and warmth but also because, under her guidance, I began to grasp Edmonton's language and culture. I learned how to communicate in English and gradually came to understand the rights and responsibilities of Canadian citizens. These lessons became a key, unlocking the door to my new life.

However, learning a new language is never easy. Despite my efforts, pronunciation remained a major hurdle and made communication frustrating. Each time I attempted to converse with native English speakers, I felt as if my words floated away, unheard and misunderstood. At times, self-doubt crept in, and the thought of giving up crossed my mind.

## Meeting Natasha: A Turning Point in Language Learning

Then, fate led me to Natasha, a teacher whose presence felt like a guiding light. With her warm smile and infinite patience, she transformed her classroom into a space of inclusivity and encouragement, where mistakes were seen as steps toward growth.

My first day in Natasha's LINC class was filled with nervous anticipation. The "icebreaker" activity required me to stand up and introduce myself — something I had been dreading. My palms grew slightly sweaty as I struggled to find the right words. But when I looked up and met Natasha's encouraging gaze, I felt a wave of reassurance. Slowly, I began to speak, piecing together sentences in broken English, and Natasha's gentle smile assured me that language learning was not really about perfection — it was about courage.

In the early days, I felt discouraged over mispronunciations and misunderstandings. At times, I feared that my words simply disappeared into thin air. But Natasha's encouraging words changed my mind set: "A language barrier doesn't mean you're incapable. It just means you need time to adjust." Her reassurance was a ray of sunshine, clearing the doubts that clouded my mind. Instead of fearing mistakes, I embraced every opportunity to speak.

Beyond teaching grammar and vocabulary, Natasha instilled hope. Under her guidance, I improved my pronunciation, gained the confidence to speak, and overcame my fear of being misunderstood. For the first time, I felt truly connected to the English language, realizing that it was not just a tool for communication, but also a bridge to belonging.

## Friendships That Cross Borders

I was not alone on my journey. In class, I met Maksym, a Ukrainian immigrant who had lived in China for many years. Maksym's fluent Mandarin became a valuable bridge, helping me to grasp complex lessons with ease. Our friendship transcended nationalities and cultures, offering me a sense of belonging in this foreign land.

One day, I found myself in conversation with a group of African Canadian workers who jokingly introduced themselves as "Chinese." Caught off guard, I hesitated for a moment before responding in jest: "I'm George. Now, I'm a Canadian too." Laughter erupted around me, and for the first time, I felt at ease speaking English. In that moment, I realized that language was more than just words, it was a way to connect with others.

## Embracing a New Life

My progress extended beyond the classroom as I actively participated in community activities, volunteering at MacEwan University, NorQuest College, and the Edmonton Food Bank. Every conversation, every act of service, brought me closer to knowing the heart of the city.

In September 2024, I received an invitation to "Coffee with Carolyn," an event where I had the chance to meet NorQuest College President Carolyn Campbell. Summoning my courage, I introduced myself in fluent English, sharing my journey as a newcomer. When Carolyn smiled and said: "George, your progress is remarkable." I felt an overwhelming sense of validation. And when she praised Natasha as an extraordinary mentor, I felt deep gratitude for her guidance.

At that moment, I understood — Natasha had not just taught me English; she had taught me how to find my place in a new society. Through language, I had not only found my voice but also my identity in Canada. I realized that my growth extended far beyond language skills. I was no longer the hesitant newcomer, afraid of speaking. Instead, I had become a confident individual, actively engaging with my new community.

## The Bridge of Language and Intent

Most mornings, I enjoy walking in my quiet neighborhood, watching the morning sun cast its rays on the trees lining the neighborhood streets, creating dappled shadows on the ground. The trees on either side of the street are thick and tall, standing like guardians of the residents. Most of the houses along the road are warm, one- or two-story homes with front porches and backyards, creating a harmonious scene. As I walk along the road, I suddenly feel a familiar sense of comfort, as though I have returned to my hometown. I start thinking that perhaps, this is what my ideal "socialist new countryside" looks like, yet I unexpectedly feel it first here in Canada.

I always wear headphones while walking, listening to recordings of "New Concept English," which makes my mornings feel fulfilling. People on the street are always friendly, greeting each other with warmth, and this pure kindness touches me.

One morning, while I was strolling, I met a gentleman. The man smiled and greeted me in not-yet-fluent Chinese, saying, "Ni Hao!" The unexpected greeting surprised and delighted me. The gentleman introduced himself as Jayme, who had immigrated to Edmonton from England over fifty years ago. He expressed a deep interest in Chinese culture and mentioned that he was born in the year of the snake. During our conversation, we found out that we lived in the same building. Jayme enthusiastically told me that he recently started dating a Chinese girlfriend named Qin Wei, whom he found very beautiful. He said he wanted to learn Chinese because of her. I smiled and mentioned that I wanted to improve my English. The two of us quickly hit it off and we agreed to meet in the evening at the building office to help each other learn our respective languages.

I shared this encounter with my teacher Natasha who was delighted to hear about it. She encouraged me, saying, "Helping each other and learning from one another is a wonderful thing."

## Teacher-Student Bond, Illuminating Hearts Together

The influence of my English teacher, Natasha, has been profound and significant in my English language journey. I always held deep respect for her. Every piece of guidance and every word of encouragement from Natasha was like an illuminating light for me whenever I faced difficulties. Looking back, I am filled with endless gratitude and warmth.

At the end of 2024, I received an email from the school inviting students to nominate an outstanding teacher for the 2024 Jaye Fredrickson Award for Teaching Excellence. Without hesitation, I nominated Natasha, out of deep admiration and gratitude. Natasha mentioned that no LINC teacher had ever won this award, but I still encouraged her to try, believing wholeheartedly that Natasha was undoubtedly the teacher most deserving of this honor.

For me, Natasha was not just a language teacher but a life mentor and a guide on my journey in Canada. Natasha deeply inspired me, making me understand that the meaning of education goes far beyond the transfer of knowledge; it is also about imbibing confidence in life and realizing one's self-worth. With Natasha's help, I not only made considerable progress in learning English but, more importantly, found the confidence and courage to integrate into Canadian society. Throughout my learning journey, I gradually realized that it is thanks to mentors like Natascha that I can keep moving forward, towards a better future.

Later, I received a letter saying that Natasha won the Jaye Fredrickson Award for Teaching Excellence. Overwhelmed with joy, I attended the award ceremony, where I had the honor of giving a heartfelt speech about Natasha's impact on my life. Standing on stage, speaking confidently in English, I felt a profound sense of achievement. My journey from a hesitant newcomer to a self-assured speaker was not just a personal victory but also a tribute to the mentors, friends, and community that had supported me along the way.

### Bridging Cultures: My New Beginnings in Canada

Striving to embrace other opportunities in Canada, I set new goals for myself both academically and personally. I enrolled in advanced English classes, striving for fluency that would allow me to re-enter the professional world. My background as a senior metro design engineer remained a core part of my identity, and I aspire to contribute my skills to Canada's infra-structure projects someday.

In early 2025, I applied for a volunteer position with the City of Edmonton's Urban Planning Department. My application was accepted, and although it was an unpaid role, it provided me with invaluable exposure to Canadian professional environments. Working alongside local engineers and planners, I was able to blend my past expertise with my growing understanding of Canadian

standards and practices. This experience not only enriched my technical knowledge but also strengthened my English communication skills in professional contexts.

Meanwhile, my friendship with Jayme flourished. Our language exchange sessions became a cherished routine, filled with laughter and mutual growth. Jayme's enthusiasm for learning Mandarin deepened his connection with Qin Wei, while my confidence in speaking English soared. We often explored Edmonton together, from strolling along the scenic North Saskatchewan River to visiting local museums and cultural festivals. Our bond is a testament to the power of cross-cultural friendships in bridging differences.

My wife, Julie, also found her own path in this new land. Drawing on her medical background, she joined a community health volunteer program where she provided support to seniors facing language barriers, much like herself. Her compassionate nature and professional knowledge made her an invaluable asset to the program. Through her volunteer work, Julie built lasting friendships and rediscovered a sense of purpose and belonging.

As the years passed, Julie and I grew more integrated into Canadian society. We celebrated traditional Chinese festivals with new friends, shared our culture through community events, and embraced Canadian holidays with equal enthusiasm. Our apartment became a warm, welcoming space filled with memories of both Shanghai and Edmonton, a true reflection of our bi-cultural journey.

Raymond Keung, "Downtown Edmonton" Watercolour 2023

# The City of Love

**By Manna Liu**

THERE IS SOMETHING ABOUT THE GENTLE RHYTHM OF WALKING ALONG the campus sidewalks that I find utterly soothing, especially during my lunch breaks. The cool, crisp air fills my lungs, and with every step, the weight of the day seems to lift.

As May gives way to June in Edmonton, the snow that once blanketed the land like a heavy veil begins to melt. Branches, once weighed down by frost, now give birth to tender buds, shyly unfurling under the newly arrived warmth of spring. In the meadow north of NorQuest College, clusters of pink and purple lingonberry buds bloom like delicate jewels. The sun shines brightly, and the sky, painted in deep hues of blue, is dotted with clouds that drift lazily across the heavens. The streets are quiet; the usual hum of the city is almost absent as if it too is savoring the tranquility of the moment. A solitary path winds through the center of the lawn, and by the side of it sits a man and a woman, both seemingly of Indigenous descent. Their backpacks rest gently at their sides. With his eyes closed, the man leans back on the bench in a state of quiet repose, while the woman, with a cigarette in hand, watches the students passing by with a contemplative gaze.

The streets outside the campus, at the intersection of 102 Avenue and 107 Street, seem like they will never be fully repaired. With the arrival of spring, the roads are once again closed off for construction. Stern barricades and bright orange cones stand in the middle of the street, halting pedestrians and vehicles. The work continues until the snow returns, only to recommence the following spring. The construction is like a cycle that never ceases, mirroring the changing of the seasons.

This year is no exception.

I am taking a walk outside the campus as usual. Across the lawn stands a red brick building, its sturdy form proudly displaying the Canadian flag at its front. It is the fire station. In front of a fire truck, a group of children gathers—one of them in a wheelchair—listening intently as a firefighter, clad in uniform, gestures toward the vehicle, explaining fire safety with the calm authority of someone who has seen it all.

I pause, struck by the tenderness of the moment. A sense of warmth stirs within me as I instinctively reach for my phone, eager to capture it. However, a teacher quietly approaches me. 'Please don't take photos of the children,' she says softly. 'They all have disabilities and are here for a tour.' Embarrassed, I immediately put my phone away, apologizing quietly.

At that very moment, in the middle of the road, a bearded man catches my eye. He stands tall, wearing an orange safety hat and a yellow vest with reflective stripes, holding a Stop sign in one hand. Bathed in the golden afternoon sunlight, his figure looks almost comical—like a character in a cartoon. Our eyes meet, and he gives me a friendly nod.

A long-forgotten memory suddenly resurfaces. When I first arrived in Canada, I spoke little English. I once chatted with a friend about how wonderful it would be to have a job that required no speaking but still paid well. With a glint of humor in his eye, he suggested I consider a job where it's simply standing on the street holding a sign—like the man I see now. High pay, no talking, just standing there silently. I laughed at the time, but deep down, I envied that simplicity. Yet, over time, I realized that envy, though temporarily comforting, leads nowhere.

When I return to the same place, the man holding the sign has already sunk into a chair and rests in the moment. His eyes follow a few workers, smoothing over the scars left on the pavement. The Stop sign, too, leans casually against a utility pole, taking its respite alongside its keeper.

I seize the moment and approach him, starting a conversation. I share how, in my early days in Canada, I envied his role in the job. He smiles warmly, gently explaining that the pay isn't as high as I had imagined and that even this job requires a certain level of English.

Yes, in a country where English is the predominant language, it's hard to imagine a job that doesn't require it. Even the illiterate need language to express their needs—to ask for help, to navigate the city, or to connect with others.

Fortunately, I decided to return to school and study English. Through this journey, I discovered a deeper calling: to work in Community Support, not only for my growth but also to help those who, like me, once felt lost as immigrants.

Over my two years of study, I navigated the challenges of the pandemic, with my internships confined to the campus. Even after graduation, I remained at the college. Yet, as time passed, I realized I had never visited any community service organization. Then, in a sudden flash of insight, the building across the street—the Navigation Center—came to mind. Why not walk in and see it for myself?

It's better to act than only to think about it. And so, I cross 103rd Avenue and arrive at the Hope Mission's Karis Centre. The memory surfaces as I recall news of the Alberta government's newly launched Navigation Centre, designed to offer much-needed support to the homeless in Edmonton. The center provides food, coffee, clothing, and even spaces for charging phones, storing personal belongings, and caring for pets. It has become an essential lifeline for the homeless and other vulnerable groups.

The building stands two stories tall. Its orange-yellow brick walls glow warmly in the sunlight. A stone bench nestles among clusters of low-growing plants, adding a touch of greenery to the serene scene. The sun spills its golden light over the people nearby, wrapping them in a tranquil embrace. A few women, likely residents, sit on the ground, their faces tilted toward the sun. Their laughter, light and unhurried, drifts through the air, mingling with the gentle rustle of leaves, infusing the moment with a quiet, timeless harmony.

In front of the building, a glass door stands framed by a black sign, its bold lettering imparting an air of solemnity: "Karis Centre." I push against the door, only to find it unyielding. As I pause in uncertainty, a man smoking a cigarette nearby notices my hesitation. With a casual gesture, he calls out, explaining that the door cannot be opened from the outside. He adds that the entrance is just around the corner.

I follow the narrow path to the other side of the building, where a simple wooden staircase leads to a metal door. Through the window, I glimpse a man seated in a chair. He notices my gaze, rises, and approaches the door. "Can I help you?" his tone cautious and courteous.

I smile gently, hoping to put him at ease, "I'm a social worker," I explain. "I've been reading the news about the Navigation Centre, and I thought I'd come by to see it, perhaps to volunteer in the future."

His face softens, and he points toward the stairway. "The basement is where the Navigation Centre is."

I descend the stairs and step into the basement, where a group of people is gathered in a spacious hall. Their focused expressions suggest they're engaged in a meeting. Quietly, I approach a table adorned with a plaque for Alberta Correctional Services. A woman named Trishana notices me, her warm smile breaking the formal atmosphere. After a brief exchange, she graciously offers to give me a tour.

At the front of the hall, two workers assist those in need. A line of people stands patiently, filling out forms. Along the walls, tables represent various services: Alberta Correctional Services, Bowline Health, The Hope Mission Service Hub, Radius, Alberta Health Services, Alberta Supports Centre, Bent Arrow (Traditional Healing Society), and Alberta Police. Trishana leads me through the rooms, which are neat and serene, with clean white linens on the beds and small spaces designated for guests' pets. The atmosphere is one of quiet compassion, a refuge from the noise of the world outside.

An hour spent wandering through the city led to a quiet epiphany. These small moments of connection, whether in a firefighter's lesson or the quiet care at the center, made me reflect deeply on the larger sense of community. It is not merely the infrastructure but the spirit of its people that imbues this city with its warmth. Though the winters are long and harsh, their icy grip cannot stifle the warmth that permeates this land.

The homeless, their eyes reflecting both struggle and hope, reminds me of a fundamental truth: community is not shaped by buildings or streets, but by the spirit that unites us. It is the force that sparks small acts of kindness—each a flicker of light in someone's darkest hour, gently guiding them forward with warmth and compassion.

This fleeting visit revealed not only a world I had never fully seen but also prompted me to reflect on my journey in this land and within the community. From the day I was adrift, struggling with a foreign language and culture, to now finding my place in education and social work, I understand that true integration into society is not merely a process of learning and adapting. It is a commitment—a commitment to embrace responsibility, to act with intention, and to extend a hand to others.

In the future, I hope to offer warmth—through my experiences, my time, or even a simple smile. Kindness is not only a way of contributing to this diverse society, but also a response to the quiet longings within me. Many of life's greatest values do not require grand gestures or elaborate plans. Sometimes, it is enough to pause, listen deeply, or offer a simple act of genuine care. These small, seemingly insignificant gestures create the tender connections that bind us.

As I walk back to campus, the sun bathes me in a golden glow. I truly realize why Chinese immigrants call it the City of Love. In addition to the fact that the city's English name sounds like the Chinese word for love, Chinese immigrants call it 'Ai Cheng' — 'City of Love' — out of deep affection for this new land. It feels like a perfect reflection of the city itself—a place where goodwill is woven into the air, and love quietly blossoms in the most unexpected places, just beneath the surface of everyday life.

Raymond Keung, "Edmonton River Valley" Watercolour

# A Blessing in Disguise:
# In Remembrance of My
# Angel Lost in Edmonton

By Rong Guo

PERHAPS, FOR A MOTHER GETTING OLD, HER CHILDREN BEING COUNTED includes not only the currently existing, but also the ones who are not fortunate enough to be given a birth. In the view of Buddhism, unborn children exist as spirits and sometimes, worse even, they roam around seeking comfort and protection from their dear mom or someone more superb. For about eighteen years, I had been haunted by regret, and remorse, whenever I thought of him or her, a miscarried child. "If I didn't ...," I cannot help replaying in my mind what had happened before its final disappearance. Today, I will try to write down the event, my guilt, my apology, and my gratitude towards the miscarried baby, who failed to appear in my life but showed me the true meaning of expecting and heralded indeed the coming of my second child. Without this accident, I might not have my second child with wholeheartedness and sincere willingness.

In mainland China, before the implementation of the new family plan policy in 2016, all couples were restricted to having only one child except if one parent was an only child themselves. This policy, issued in 1982, was strictly carried out in cities among people working in governments or formal public institutions. If a rule were broken, jobs would be ended, and couples would have to become casual laborers without regular and secure benefits. For this reason, few people in the system would risk their job and future, and most people of child-bearing age restrained their temptation to have a second child.

In this situation, people obsessed with strong traditional thoughts of having a male child would try their best to play with the policy in order to fulfill their dream. Thus, various stories were displayed on the stage, some fantastically shocking and monstrous. Of course, examples exist of people ignoring the rule. They would rather pay heavy fines in order to have more children. For instance, Zhang Yimou, one of the most famous film directors in China, paid almost 7.5 million RMB to have three children, two boys and one girl. In contrast, my story was rather plain and not that eventful.

When I announced that I was preparing to have a baby, my mother-in-law, who used to be a doctor in my county hospital, urged me to have a kind of medicine which, according to her, would increase the probability of conceiving a boy. I rejected her proposal immediately, stating that I would not risk the health of my child for the purpose of having a boy. I told my husband that I would not have a baby until he and his mother let go of their obsessions that only boys were welcomed.

However, my parents-in-law never truly gave up their efforts. After my first daughter was born, they insisted on adopting a baby boy on behalf of my husband. I protested strongly, declaring that I would divorce their son if they persisted. Noticing my resolve, they put aside their decision very reluctantly.

In 2004, I came to Edmonton as an international student. My mother-in-law, knowing from somewhere-only-God-knows that there was no family plan policy in Canada, started again to nudge her son to have another child. I was angry that she could reach across the ocean and continent to interfere in my life. Perhaps, being rebellious at the core of my mind, I refused to have another child not because of the hardship of raising a child, but because of the interference and manipulation of my parents-in-law. I made up my mind. I would not have another child even in sparsely populated Canada where no official agencies would supervise and control childbearing.

Unexpectedly, at the beginning of winter term in 2007, I found that I was pregnant. At the time, I was preparing for my PhD dissertation, and I was convinced that the coming of a new baby would certainly postpone my graduation. I contacted Woman's Health Options in Edmonton, the only one available for abortion services in Northern Alberta and made an appointment. It was arranged, fortunately or unfortunately, twenty days later. The receptionist concluded by saying the following remarks, "Don't come if you change your mind; you don't need to call us either." I could not help recalling the convenience in China, where abortion services were provided everywhere, and no appointments were required.

During the waiting time, I prayed to God, "You are kind, and you are almighty. Please take away this child. I really don't want to have it!" Two weeks later, along with the continuation of pregnancy reactions, I had gradually accepted the fact and gave up the idea of an abortion. I did not go to the centre on the appointed date. Yet, a tragedy was approaching beyond my awareness.

One Monday afternoon, my husband had a day off and he accompanied me to walk in the Snow Valley. Time passed quickly, and soon it was five o'clock, the time to pick up my daughter. We took a shortcut. It was short, but we had to climb up a steep slope. I had some difficulty, and he decided to pull me up. Out of breath, I asked him to leave me alone, assuring him that I could climb myself. Yet, out of his consideration or responsibility as a husband, perhaps, he insisted and continued to pull me straight up. The entire process lasted for about fifteen minutes, and it left me completely breathless. Then, he walked to Lansdowne Child Care, and I walked home in Michener Park.

The next morning, I noticed some bloodstain, but I took no notice, subconsciously believing that the child was given by God and that it would not leave easily. When the bleeding continued and the color of blood changed from dark to fresh red, I was a little upset and called my obstetrician, who arranged an urgent ultrasound.

Friday morning, on the appointed time, I went to the ultrasound centre. The technician welcomed me with a smiling face. She recognized me. As it turned out, her son and my daughter were in the same daycare. I knew her son, but I did not remember her. My tension did ease up a little. I laid down, and she began to manage the machine. Almost right away, I noticed that her facial expression changed, but she did not say anything. Instead, she turned to me, saying cautiously like a whisper, "I would find a doctor and let that doctor explain to you." My heart sank a little, but I was still not entirely without hope.

A burly and serious-looking male doctor entered the room. He had a quick look at the screen, and said matter-of-factly and with great firmness, "Your baby cannot be kept. You need to go to the Alex." I did not know where and what the Alex was, but I caught his message. My heart pounded and tears rolled down my face uncontrollably. I tried to stay calm, but my voice quivered as I spoke. Seeing that I was so upset, the technician took the initiaves. She called a taxi and jotted down the address of the hospital. Then she hugged me, walked me all the way to the ground floor, and made sure I got in the cab.

The taxi driver, a middle-aged Indian man with a white turban, was very kind. He drove slowly and tried to avoid any disturbances. We came to the Royal Alexandra Hospital in about twenty minutes. The receptionist at the front desk recorded my information, and I was taken to a ward. Lying on the bed, I could not control my trembling. The room was bathed in sunshine, but I still felt cold. The nurse brought me an extra blanket, which was freshly dried and still warm. For the whole afternoon, I asked for three extra blankets in total. I remember till today the warmth they brought to me, even if just for a short while. Knowing my situation, the nurse tried to console me. She gently wiped tears off my face, soothing me by stating that miscarried babies are usually unhealthy, and that I was still young and would surely have babies in the future.

Due to the shortage of beds, my operation was postponed repeatedly until six o'clock in the afternoon. From 12:30 to 5 o'clock, I lay on the bed, having nothing to do. My cell phone did not work while I was at the hospital, and I could not contact anyone. Moreover, in the morning rush, I did not bring any books with me, assuming that I would return home soon. Thinking seemed to become the only thing I could do; not until then, did I have time to ruminate my behaviors. Why didn't I insist on walking slowly by myself? Why didn't I take actions at the beginning when I noticed the blood? I even wondered why God didn't help me keep the child. Wasn't the child coming from God? Was God disciplining me for not cherishing the gift given by him? Questions collided in my mind. I had no answers, but I could not help blaming God and blaming myself.

Finally, the time came, and I was transferred to another building for the operation. The moment I got out of the lift, I saw a young lady on a wheelchair with her baby held to her breast. A fleeting thought went through my mind, "Her baby is alive, but my baby left." The lady will never know that her image with a baby to her breast would bring such a strong impact to me. I envied her. "How I wish it was me who sits there!" Never did I have such an intense feeling that I would like to have a baby, my own baby.

The operation lasted for about half an hour. With the effects of anesthesia, I actually felt nothing. When I woke up, I was already back in the ward bed. My husband and his friend were waiting. I was actually missing for more than nine hours. For a full two hours, they had been searching for me, from the emergency department of the U of A hospital to the ward of the Alex. They were relieved to find me but knew nothing of what a long day I had experienced.

Thanks to the inspiring image of the young mother and child, I began to prepare actively for pregnancy, completely different from my previous rebellious attitude. I even wonder, was it God, who listened to my prayer and took away my child in order to change my mindset? Perhaps, people only learn to cherish when they experience loss. In any case, my second daughter came in 2008, and I was careful about the whole pregnancy. I dared not take any risk and I followed exactly the instruction of my obstetrician. Never did I show any aversion or antipathies during my pregnancy. Subconsciously, I began a new respect for life, which is not something durable and not easy to lose. Children might be from God, and they should be loved and cherished; otherwise, they might be taken away.

Nowadays, we humans have achieved great progress in terms of science and technology. We launched rockets to Mars, and we landed human beings on the moon. We have produced so many different advanced devices. Yet, one thing is still magical, that is the creation of life. Though successful cases are here and there, it is still impossible to understand why babies do not come even when all conditions are met. Life is magic and deserves our deep and full respect.

The disappearance of my miscarried baby indeed makes me feel regret and remorse, but it is also a blessing in disguise. It teaches me the lesson of respecting life. I also appreciate the kindness of the Ultrasound technician, the taxi driver, the nurse, the young and humorous surgeon, and all the staff in the operating room, who comforted me, encouraged me and supported me while I underwent this dark moment in my life. In retrospect, I changed from a rebellious woman to a loving and cherishing mother. All of this is owed to the accident that I may have caused myself. By putting this story on paper, I hope, the unborn baby, my angel lost in Edmonton, will feel my love and accept my apology; in my writing, I wish, this child, my angel, will obtain a life he or she failed to have. Hopefully, one day in the future, we will meet again in the heaven created and promised by God and my expectation.

# discovering
## *belonging*

"Belonging is not about fitting in, it's about being accepted for who you are." - Brené Brown

# Stories Bind us Together

**By Goldwin McEwen**

WHAT IS EDMONTON? JUST A PLACE WE CALL HOME; A PLACE OF interest where visitors roam? A menagerie of mementoes, old made new? Meeting places made of art, red roofs and tall green structures pushing against blue? Like all places, this city has buildings and statues and tributes and fossils displayed. Threads of tales woven into a braid.

Chinatown, for example, is but one strand of Edmonton intertwined with many. Stories as colourful as any are captured in resin as lions guard an invisible gate. One of countless stories combined with those from other places and twisted into rugged rope that holds us all together. This tether of tales is formed with the strength of legends from many lands. Not all are myths or magic but each separate strands. Stories entwined in time until we ask what's yours; what's mine?

All of Edmonton is people, some old, some new. All keeping our traditions in everything we do. People accentuate and educate. We participate and elevate to respectfully remember **we are the same**. Bound by the twine made of stories, we combine threads from life on a turbulent sea. Moored, we feel safe in a place of our own. This place, Edmonton, is our home. We are not just visitors here to roam.

Raymond Keung, "AGA" Watercolour 2023

# History Lesson

## By Paul Fujishige

WHEN I WAS FIRST HIRED TO WORK WITH PEOPLE WITH DISABILITIES, I viewed it as merely a job to earn income. I had never attempted this kind of work before. It was intriguing and a bit scary since I had little familiarity.

I was a student at the University of Manitoba in 1979 and in need of a summer job to help pay tuition. Other job prospects had not worked out and my choices had dwindled down to one. The Society for Manitobans with Disabilities was looking for male camp counselors. I was offered the job at the interview and reluctantly accepted. I was nervous about what I was getting into.

At that time, my knowledge of disability was limited to my family's world view. My family had a typical Japanese Canadian attitude. People with disabilities were portrayed as needy and dependent.

The Japanese in general viewed disability with pity or shame. Although attitudes have become more enlightened in recent years, there is still the tendency to keep persons with disabilities hidden and out of sight as much as possible.

In my Japanese Canadian community in Winnipeg, the disability label was rarely applied to family members who would fit the criteria today. Families would close ranks around their family member like a cocoon. The person would be treated as family but would not be expected to participate or contribute. They were silent members, seen but not heard.

I did not see any connection of disability to my racial background and history. As I mentioned, initially it was just a job, not a career or anything personal that would impact my life. Over the years, my perspective changed dramatically, and I pursued a life-long career in the disability support field. It fulfilled both professional and personal purposes in my life.

In 1991 I moved to Edmonton and was hired to work with a local not-for-profit agency.

I was introduced to Tom. He was an older gentleman - tall and lanky, with a neatly trimmed moustache and a twinkle in his eye. He greeted me warmly with a broad smile and a firm handshake. Tom did not appear to have a disability and with his well-developed social skills, it was hard to believe he had been institutionalized.

Tom owned his own home and had a roommate. I would learn that this was an unusual situation, since most people who receive the Assured Income for the Severely Handicapped (AISH) assistance (an Alberta government pension program), did not receive enough money to be homeowners.

Tom had recently retired and was interested in finding social activities in his community. Tom joined the local Senior Citizens Club. He was keen to sign up for the Darts Group.

We arrived at the Club and were met by Isabel, the Director who I sensed was a bit nervous. Her words were reassuring and encouraging but there was something unsettling to me. She asked questions that seemed to me to be unrelated to playing darts.

It reminded me of when I was a teenager, and someone would ask me about my Japanese heritage when it had little relevance to what we were discussing. This would always bother me.

Tom participated in his first Darts Group and loved it. He thought everyone was friendly and he felt accepted by his peers. I sensed something different.

The other Seniors were polite and reserved. Tom was new to the group and there was always the getting-to-know-you phase when a new person joins an established group. Tom did not seem to see any problem. He felt accepted and was able to play an activity he enjoyed.

A few weeks passed. I received a call from Isabel to meet with her about Tom, without Tom present. Alarm bells went off in my head. Isabel fidgeted as she explained that some of the members were uncomfortable with Tom. She could not pinpoint any specific incident that had occurred. Some of the seniors had negative preconceptions of people with mental disability labels and were fearful that Tom would do something "strange."

When I reminded her about the Senior's Club non-discrimination policy, her eyes grew wide. She assured me that they were following the policy, and she was trying to accommodate everyone. She suggested that it would be easier for all concerned to work out an alternative – Tom could come at another time on his own or a separate dart group for people with disabilities could be formed.

This reminded me of my family's difficulty after the bombing of Pearl Harbor during the Second World War. I recalled hearing about the hatred they faced from others simply because they were Japanese Canadians, not because of anything they had done. I remember my mother describing the pain of rejection from people she thought were her friends.

After being forced out of their homes in Vancouver by the Federal and British Columbia Governments, my family was escorted by police, first to an internment camp and eventually to resettlement in Winnipeg. My family had difficulty renting a home and getting work. Prior to their arrival, they were already stereotyped and characterized as sneaky, dirty, and untrustworthy.

After 80 years, the discriminations suffered by my family and now Tom, made me wonder how much progress society has made in accepting the differences in people. Tom's situation in discussion showed me that we still have a long way to go.

I told Isabel I would talk to Tom and get back to her.

As I sat down with Tom, I tried to think what my mother would say. She believed that if someone did not like you because of what you looked like, the best strategy was to turn away and avoid making waves. If you showed someone that you were a "model citizen," you might be eventually accepted.

She would remind me that my grandfather's defiance of internment got him jailed and he was shipped to Winnipeg with the rest of the family anyway. In my mother's eyes, making waves did not lead to any good outcomes.

As I suspected, Tom had no interest in making waves, even if it was his right to participate in darts. In fact, he soured on the idea of even going to the Senior Citizen's Club again.

Understandably, he did not want to go to a place where he was not accepted.

As frustrated and angry as I felt, my job was to support Tom and honour his wishes. We stopped going to the club.

As I got to know Tom better, his experiences frequently reminded me of my family's experiences, albeit under quite different circumstances.

Tom was ostracized by Alberta society because of his disability, through no fault of his own. He was taken from his family in the 1960's and moved to Michener Centre in Red Deer. Through the "expert" advice of Government officials and physicians, his family had little choice. They were told to forget about him and to move on with their lives.

Similarly, my family was involuntarily removed from Vancouver. Politicians were fearful that the Japanese living on the west coast would assist Japan in the invasion of Canada. Fanning the flames of fear, most citizens demanded that the government act quickly. The decision was made to send the Japanese (including those born in Canada) to internment camps in the interior of B.C. Promises were made that property would be returned once the war had ended. The real goal, however, was deportation to Japan.

While we would have good conversations about our mutual experiences, Tom avoided talking about the many years he lived in Michener Centre other than to say it was a "bad place." I told Tom that my parents also did not talk about their experience during the war, and it was only my research many years later that I learned details about their forcible removal, confinement, and resettlement.

Tom learned, as my family did, to go along with those in authority and trust that they were looking out for their best interests.

The result of that compliance?

My family lost their property and their possessions. Despite the promise of return after the war ended, everything was sold off with no compensation provided. Our extended family was split up and scattered throughout the country. The Japanese Canadian community in Vancouver was changed forever.

Tom's suffering was greater. He spent decades living in a crowded dorm with up to 50 other men. He had no freedom to leave and had a regimented routine. Worse, he was sterilized without consent or even knowledge that it was happening.

Justice did occur in subsequent years that partly compensated for the past. In 1988, the Canadian Government apologized to Japanese Canadians for internment and provided individual compensation of $21,000 plus additional millions to promote racial tolerance.

Beginning in 1996, Michener Centre's victims of involuntary sterilization received an apology from the Provincial Government and compensation of between $75,000 to $100,000. This gave Tom the means to purchase his own home.

Both forms of compensation, of course, would not undo the harm that was done by the State.

Over my forty-year career in disability services, I deeply appreciated and cherished my work, especially with people like Tom. Although everyone who were "clients" of the system had a clinical disability label, it was rarely mentioned and was of little relevance. They were all accepting of the other's differences. In my case, I was appreciated and accepted for who I was, not how I looked.

People were honest. They would speak their minds without hesitation. Trustworthiness was important to me, and I was never disappointed.

Above all, I was struck by the positive outlook that most had about their lives, despite some harrowing experiences. Most had faith that their future would be bright. It was a lot easier for me to think of a hopeful future with role models like that around me.

There were times throughout my career when my beliefs and heritage were tested. The most vivid experience happened in that first job in 1977 when I was a summer student, working at a camp for adults with disabilities. I was told to intervene in a most uncomfortable situation

Bob and Wendy were a loving couple whose only opportunity to get together was one week a year at this camp. It was the night before the end of camp and there was always a farewell dance and party at the main hall.

Bob was in my cabin group and towards the end of the evening I noticed he was not with us. Ron, the camp director, told me to check the cabin.

I walked into the cabin and heard two people rustling about. It was Bob and I assumed Wendy was there as well. I returned to the party and asked Ron what to do.

He instructed me to ask Bob if he had any "protection." This was upsetting to me as I felt I was already intruding. However, I assumed that the person in authority with greater experience knew better than I, so I returned to the cabin.

Bob assured me he had protection. Relieved that he was not offended, I reported back to my superior. Tom was not satisfied and asked if I saw the "rubber." I was sent back again for further interrogation.

At that point, my anxiety and shame reached my limit. I had already intruded in their privacy and trampled on their dignity. They were familiar with these breaches and were not offended. I, however, was disturbed and felt that regardless of my professional responsibility, I would go no further. I returned to Tom and reported that I had seen the "rubber."

Sometimes if you truly see others as equals, you resist taking actions that do not seem right, even if there are "experts" and supervisors who sanction those actions.

Looking back, I now see that my career path was not an accident. My family's experience prepared me for my life's work and instilled in me the desire to help others in a way that encouraged self-determination and promoted dignity.

Injustice can appear in many forms. I had the unique opportunity to see the world through different lenses and to use that knowledge in a constructive way.

In the end, we are more alike than different, and we all deserve respect, especially by those in authority. I learned and relearned those lessons throughout my career. I continue to put it into practice every day. In our world today, those attributes are needed more than ever.

Raymond Keung, "Bird" Watercolour

# Why Do I Love Dandelions?

## By Ting Pimentel-Elger

WHERE ARE THE PEOPLE? I ASKED MY THEN-BOYFRIEND-NOW HUSBAND upon picking up my luggage. Arriving from a congested city of almost fifteen million people... And then here I am.

I love the spaciousness, and I just smiled when my then boyfriend complained about the horrible, two-minute traffic in *Deadmonton*!

I picked little yellow flowers and put them in the vase. No, they are not daisies- they are weeds! I was told

*I really don't care; I say they're beautiful and they're edible too. -*

I can spend hours in the lovely and quaint Old Strathcona library and hoard a ridiculous number of books which is not allowed where I come from.

I will rush crossing 104 and Whyte Ave, admire the window display of a little plaid shirt, which I purchase for a sale price of almost six dollars at the Army Navy Club.

Fast forward 2004-I'm driving my first car and stepped on the brake when the traffic light turned amber. Suddenly, a white, old man overtook and gave me the finger! I see his mouth saying, "Go back to where you came from!" I pulled over on the side of the road, feel my face shriek, and I bawled, my whole body started shaking. Feelings of frustration, self-loathing, bitter anger hit me. I miss my old self in Manila, where I belonged, where I can make mistakes and still be ok. Wait, was I in the wrong?

*Pull those ugly, yellow weeds! They do not belong in a perfect green golf landscape.*

For the fourth time, I tell them I AM FILIPINO! Then not realizing, after ten years, I will be that hyphenated person...

*Am I turning into that noxious weed?*

I will be calling my daughter *coconut*; you know that kind that is white inside, but brown outside. Immediately, I felt that pang of guilt.

I will stop translating in my head from English to Tagalog then to English and will say, for sure, instead of *Oo nga!*

I will drop the spoon and use fork only.... which I now use both spoon and fork again.

Until I felt that tugging in my heart- *who are you? Sino ka?* That deep longing to connect with my roots.

Entering the little forests in the river valley is like bathing in heavenly greenish sunshine – one day they seem to be all dressed in white, smelling of fresh pine and spruce.

And oh, my - hear that "chickadee dee dee dee."

*The birds nourish themselves by eating dandelions.*

And look at the big, pink cotton candy skies.... I can stay here forever.

Covid hits – I am forced to pick up the pen and the brush and the upcycled canvas and pizza box – I meet kind, friendly Filipinos that are established in Edmonton, who are accepting, funny, and well, a bit crazy and artsy like me.

*Dandelion is not only used as functional medicine, but it can also be used in arts and crafts.*

Then I realize that Edmonton, my Edmonton, is where I first planted my garden of dill, spinach, marigold, nasturtium, poppies and that giant, ant attracting peony.

I manipulate the dry, hard stubborn clayish soil- with abundance of sunshine and my own vermi compost–they thrive and still growing...coping... evolving...

Like me.

It is here in my Edmonton that I will hang my "Manila Traffic" abstract work in AGA and in my local Art Gallery.

It is here in my Edmonton that I will have my first public poetry reading and yes, I was trembling in fear, but I did it anyway and people were kind and receptive.

It is here in my Edmonton, that I will teach my first yoga and meditation class and learn how to cope with my anxiety (and with tons of therapy)

I hear a quote from E. E. Cummings:

*i carry your heart with me.*
*i am never without it anywhere...*
*i go you go, my dear*

Then it dawned on me—

That is exactly what my *Lola* will say - my dead ancestors will tell me—

It is ok, *Anak*.

Oh, you are from Edmonton, eh? Is it true that it is...

Edmonton is alive and kicking - feel the Edmonton Folk Fest or the Fringe vibe and grab some fresh micro greens and that organic rosemary garlic sausage from OSFM[1]! But you got to be there by 8 in the morning otherwise they'll be gone.

And yes, I still pick dandelions.

For my tea, for my bath and for my art!

I live in *SherWHITE* Park now though.

---

1       Old Strathcona Farmers Market

Jared Quinney, "The River Valley" Acrylic on Canvass

# Where do I come from?

**By Ting Pimentel-Elger**

In a place white as snow-
People ask me "Where are you from?"
I emigrated here from a third world country.
Before the Twin Towers fell...

But where I come from, they don't ask this –
They embrace people white, black, brown
and all kinds of mixes and races.
Someone asked me – enunciating every syllable,

"Whaat ees your neym?" to my face –
I thought "I am not deaf.
I do understand, speak and write English."
But of course, I didn't say it out loud –

Who am I to say that I am just an immigrant,
a forever foreigner here.
So what if I have taken an oath to the Queen
I have never seen.
Yes, I do exercise my right of suffrage!
Yes, I do own a house and pay mortgage!
Yes, I converse in English and choose not to speak my
     language.

As if I can hide my skin color, renouncing my heritage
My heart still belongs to where I come from-
My ancestors will be turning in their graves-
I must be strong and brave!

I will not be ashamed of who I am
and what I have become.
I will be proud
and speak eloquently with my accent!
You know what that means?
I speak more than one language!

I have travelled through the desert
and mountains of garbage.
I have survived poverty
as well as prosperity.
I was raised to have respect
and integrity.

My aging grandparents made us promise.
They want to be buried in their birthland –
Where they will forever be laid to rest.

Where did they come from?
And where are they going?

# On Stage

**By Roxanne Riemer**

THE STAGE LIGHTS ENFOLDED ME AS I STOOD AMONG MY FELLOW performers. The hum of the awaiting audience pressed against the curtain as the final note hung in the air. My heart pounded in sync with the closing notes of the music, and I felt the weight of my headdress as a constant reminder of the journey that led me here. I was no longer an outsider—I belonged.

—

It had been just over a year since I first stepped into the world of Beijing Opera. I met Peggy Yu, the President of the Edmonton Beijing Opera Association, through a very dear friend who was encouraging my daughter to perform a song at a Chinese Culture Youth Talent Competition. This was especially unique because both my daughter and I are not Chinese. We are Caucasian but have taken a special interest in exploring Chinese culture and learning the Mandarin language. Peggy set aside special times in her day multiple times to introduce and teach a Beijing Opera song to my daughter, focusing on pronunciation and flow, incorporating thoughtful hand gestures, and delivering the opera voice to her audience. As my daughter and I became increasingly fascinated by the precision of movement, the intricate melodies, and the stunningly detailed costumes, Peggy invited and welcomed us without hesitation and with wide, open arms.

At first, it was my daughter who was most involved in learning the art of Beijing Opera. I learned to dress her in the layers of delicate silks, paint her face with the white and pale pink makeup, and fasten the headdress securely on her head. At first,

I was the outsider looking in- supporting from the sidelines, captivated by the beauty and discipline of the art form.

The more I watched, the more I was drawn in—especially by Peggy. Peggy was more than just the president; she was the heart of every performance. I had seen her perform multiple times. Her voice soared with confidence and power, commanding the stage effortlessly. Watching her perform was mesmerizing—not just for her skill but for her unwavering determination. She orchestrated entire events with precision, ensuring every detail was perfect. She had done this time and time again, and yet each performance carried the same passion, the same commitment. Her strength and kindness left a lasting impression on me. It was an honor and a privilege when Peggy invited me to perform on stage with her and the Edmonton Beijing Opera group at a Spring Gala in 2024.

In the many weeks and months leading up to the performance, I immersed myself in every aspect of Beijing Opera. I learned the techniques—how to step with grace, how to hold the props with purpose, and how to channel emotions through every movement. My teachers, experienced performers who had trained for years, gently corrected my form, demonstrating again and again until I got it just right.

Every movement told a story—a flick of the wrist, a measured step, a graceful turn. One of the biggest challenges was learning the distinct walk of the opera. Unlike natural movement, it was controlled, deliberate—each step gliding just above the floor, each turn executed with precision. "Feel the rhythm, 一·二·三· 四, one, two, three, four," Peggy would say, watching me closely.

Holding the props was another challenge. Whether it was a delicate fan, a long flowing sleeve, or an ornamental staff, each item had to be incorporated into the performance with intention. A simple flick of the wrist could express joy, sorrow, or triumph. I had to learn the subtle language of each movement.

The night before the performance, I barely slept. My mind raced with last-minute worries—what if I forgot a step? What if I tripped? But as I entered the theater the next day, those fears were replaced with quiet determination. This was about more than just getting every step right; it was about being part of something meaningful.

Inside the dressing room, the heavy scent of makeup filled the air. We shared snacks and stories, getting to know one another in the long hours of preparation. The process took at least five hours, during which we laughed, encouraged one another, and exchanged unique experiences. Everyone helped each other dress, securing layers of silk, adjusting ornate accessories, and carefully applying makeup. The headdresses, heavy and intricate, were fastened tightly to our heads, their weight pressing down on me until dizziness set in by the end of the night.

My reflection in the mirror stared back at me—eyes framed by bold black lines, cheeks dusted with a pale pink hue, and lips painted delicately in red. Months of practice had led to this moment, and now, standing among my fellow performers, I felt a mix of exhilaration and nervous anticipation. The transition from practice to performance was daunting. The stage was set at the Edmonton Winspear Centre. Inside the theatre lay a sea of darkness where hundreds of audience members sat. As I stood in the stage wings, waiting for my cue, my palms grew damp, my breath came in shallow bursts. The vastness of the stage stretched before me, its emptiness daunting until the music called me forward.

The music swelled, and I stepped forward. For a heartbeat, I hesitated. Then, the rhythm took hold, my body responding as if guided by something greater than myself. The fear dissolved. I moved, not as an outsider, but as part of the story, part of the art, part of the Edmonton Beijing Opera family.

As the final note resonated through the theater, the audience erupted into applause. The blackness beyond the stage flickered with camera flashes, and I caught sight of Peggy's approving smile. Beside me, my fellow performers beamed with pride, their eyes alight with the same sense of fulfillment I felt in my chest.

And then, all too quickly, it was over. The final bow. The thunderous applause. The triumphant walk backstage, where we laughed, embraced, and celebrated our shared accomplishment. It was more than a performance to me; it was a testament to the power of inclusivity, of cultural exploration, of finding a home in unexpected places.

Peggy caught my eye as we stepped backstage, her approving nod saying more than words ever could. Around me, my fellow performers laughed and embraced, our shared triumph filling the air. I had started this journey as a guest—but I had found a home.

I joined the Edmonton Beijing Opera Club to learn, to explore, to challenge myself. In the end, it has given me something far greater. It had given me a community, a sense of togetherness that transcended language and background. As I stepped out of the theater into the crisp Edmonton night, still humming the melodies that had filled the air just moments before, I felt a newfound connection—not just to the art, but to the vibrant tapestry of cultures that make up my city, my home. This was more than a performance; it was a doorway, inviting me to continue exploring, preserving, and celebrating the rich heritage that unites us all.

**Photo credit:
Roxanne Riemer**

# my roots,
# *my community*

"Never forget your roots, it's the foundation that builds your existence and the secret to your future." - Cherry Mpio

"If you want to go quickly, go alone. If you want to go far, go together." — African Proverb

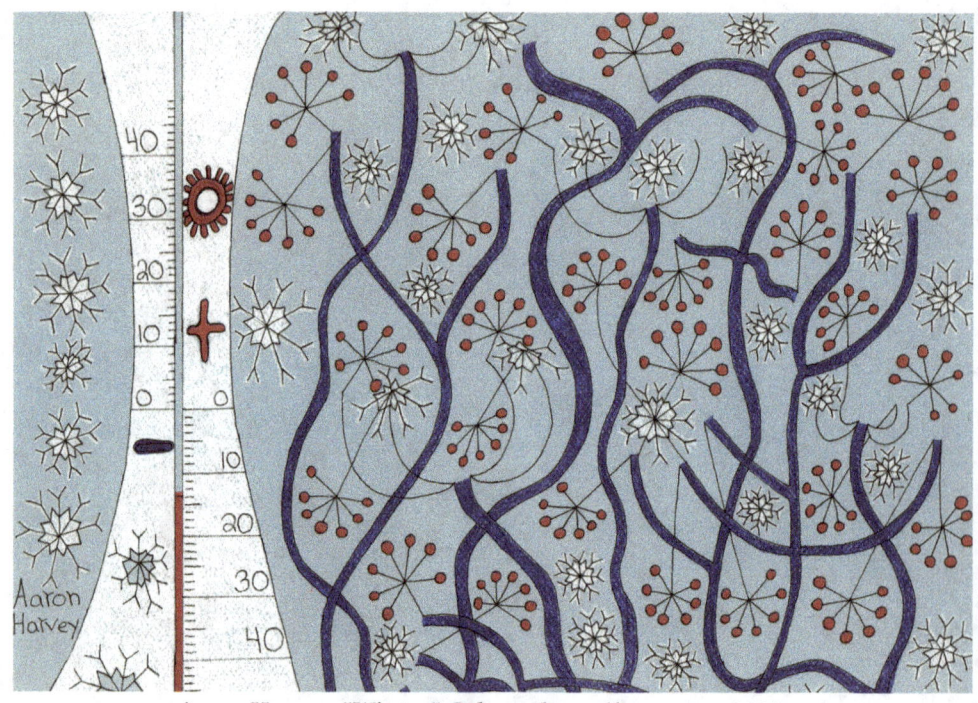

Aaron Harvey, "Winter" Coloured pencil on paper, 2021

# Roots to Resilience: A Ukrainian Childhood in Edmonton

By Launa-Rae Linaker

It's Christmas again. Edmonton transforms into a glistening wonderland in winter. When the snow is deep and the air crisp and the city seems wrapped in a hushed magic I remember my Ukrainian roots. For more than 100 years my family has been part of this great province and this wonderful country. I never have to wonder who I am. I know. I am a Canadian of Ukrainian decent. It all began with advertisements asking for families to come and farm.

The newspaper ads were compelling: *"The Last Best West" and "Land of Opportunity: Come to Canada."* These ads resulted in a substantial influx of Ukrainian settlers, who played a crucial role in developing Canada's agricultural sector and contributing to its cultural diversity. Several waves of Ukrainian immigration began in the late 19th century, with the first settlers arriving in 1891. Many established themselves in Alberta rural areas, particularly in east-central Alberta, forming the Edna-Star settlement.

It is important to acknowledge that Ukrainian settlers, like other European immigrants, farmed land that Indigenous Peoples had lived on and stewarded for generations. They were unaware of Canadian government treaties and policies that made this land available to settlers while restricting Indigenous ways of life. Despite this, my family's journey followed this path.

My grandfather, Paul Fundytus, arrived in Alberta in 1901 when he was three, and his family farmed near Mundare, where

Ukrainian traditions flourished, and a strong entrepreneurial spirit took root. He met my grandmother, Nellie Hawryluk, the youngest of six children, and they built a life together. They had one child, my father. Like many rural families, my grandfather moved his family to Edmonton when my dad was five. They were drawn by economic opportunities, education, and the promise of a more centralized life. They brought with them the resilience and values that had defined their rural existence. The resilience and values that are a large part of me.

By the late 1940s, the Ukrainian settlers had built a strong presence in northeast Edmonton, shaping the cultural and economic landscape of the city. Many farmers transformed their entrepreneurial mindset from farming to business, opening thriving Ukrainian-owned establishments that contributed to Edmonton's multicultural tapestry and downtown growth. My grandmother, a woman of boundless energy, opened Nellie's Cafe in 1949 at 9662 - 105 Avenue, though she closed it a year later and took a position at Zenith Cafe on Jasper Avenue, where she cooked up to 100 meals in an hour. Downtown Edmonton was a bustling centre. Later, she became the first female manager at Zellers, overseeing the ladies' department until she passed away in 1974.

Losing my grandmother affected me deeply, but I still cherish her memory as a powerful motivator. Even today, I see her warm smile urging me to enjoy the day. She accompanies me silently as I work through questions weighing heavily on my mind and my world closes in around my shoulders.

It was not the same when I was six years old, when the world felt immense, especially at Christmas. My family was steeped in Ukrainian Christmas traditions centered around food rather than religion. My Baba, who lived with us, began preparations in early December. These traditions and moments of gathering and sharing were the heart of our family. I only had one brother but sixteen cousins, and they were my siblings at this time of year. We loved gathering on Christmas Eve, sneaking cookies before racing through the twelve traditional dishes so we could finally leave the formal grown-ups at the table to play.

I also eagerly anticipated our annual trip from our cozy home in the Cromdale community to the heart of downtown Edmonton. We stayed warm by bundling in scarves, mittens, and warm coats, before going out into the crisp night. It was a quick ride on the bus. As we approached Jasper Avenue, the city's main thoroughfare, my eyes grew wide, as I took it all in. The festive decorations stretched across light posts, and garlands framed shop entrances. Twinkling lights led the way. Hopping off the trolly bus, the street felt alive with the crunch of snow beneath my boots, and each breath hung in the air like a whispered spell.

Our first stop was always the Hudson's Bay Company department store, where my dad worked, it was a beacon of holiday cheer. The department store held a special place in my heart. It symbolized the joy and wonder of the holiday season with its grand window displays and festive atmosphere. Every year in December, its windows transformed into miniature worlds of wonder. I would press up against the cold glass, getting lost in my imagination. There was one display I remember that brought Santa's workshop to life. The tiny elves were hammering and painting with such precision, yet they might look up at any moment. I imagined them lifting their heads, their eyes twinkling and giving me a wink. I remember the peaceful winter village display, where ice skaters glided across a frozen pond, their scarves trailing behind them, imprinting the magic of winter upon me. These scenes were more than decorations; they were stories woven in light and motion, igniting a sense of magic that stayed with me long after we left.

After immersing ourselves in the enchanting displays and other festivities, we would go to the Zellers Skillet counter, where I always ordered a strawberry milkshake. No shake has ever tasted as rich, cold, or perfectly sweet. I remember sitting on the counter stool, swirling my legs, surrounded by the certainty of safety and belonging. In these moments, I felt a deep connection with my family. A sense of shared experience, a ritual, which bound us together.

Over 50 years have passed since my childhood days, but the spirit of those downtown adventures lives inside me. Christmas remains my favourite time of year because it brings people together to share food and laughter. While there is no longer a Hudson's Bay department store with decorated windows, I still feel the same wide-eyed excitement I felt on those cold December nights, with my face pressed against the glass, dreaming in the glow of a holiday window. These memories and experiences are a part of me, as is the resilient and entrepreneurial spirit of my ancestors, shaping who I am and how I see the world.

# Building My Community in Edmonton

By Pravatika Rai

## The Initial Shock

ON A SUNNY AFTERNOON IN OCTOBER 2019, AS WE STEPPED OFF THE plane, my daughter and I immediately felt the crisp Autumn air in Edmonton. It was an energizing change from our warm homeland of Nepal. Eyes sparkling with excitement, we took in the unfamiliar sights and sounds of the Edmonton International Airport: the freshly brewed coffee from Tim Hortons, the perfectly lined taxis at the airport parking, and the mix of faces from people around the world.

As we walked through the bustling terminal, our hearts pounded with eagerness for the opportunities that awaited us in Canada. We had left behind our familiar world of narrow streets and street side vendors, a world full of loved ones, and cherished memories like the neighborhood playground with familiar noises of the kids playing Cricket, all left far behind to embark on a future filled with new adventures and endless possibilities.

With each step, a mix of nervousness and excitement grew. This was a leap of faith, a chance to start anew. As we claimed the luggage and headed towards the exit, we could not help but feel a sense of wonder. What adventures lay ahead?

The initial days in Edmonton were full of strange experiences, for example, going to Superstore just to get a pack of salt. Back in Nepal, we have small shops in every street selling everyday items. Oftentimes, if we see someone from the next-door neighbor going to shop, we ask them to buy a thing or two for us as well, to save us from running the errand. It is uncommon for us to run into big grocery stores for every single item. Walking long extended aisles just to look for our chili spice 'magaz' (melon seeds) was also challenging. Such experiences remind us we are in a vastly different world. The "newness to the land" proved to be difficult.

Cultural adjustments were equally demanding. The customs, social norms, and pace of life were vastly different from what we knew. We were used to a closely bonded society, where everyone knows everyone in the neighborhood. If a guest arrives at one household with a pack of sweets, the sweets reach every single house in the neighborhood. Our initial excitement in being in Edmonton gradually gave way to a sense of isolation and homesickness. We yearned for the well-known comforts of our homeland, the warmth of familiar faces, the warm smile from grandmother when we return home after work, the talking from the bubbly child of the neighborhood, and the taste of "momo," Nepal's favorite dish

Despite the challenges, my daughter and I persevered. We enrolled in language classes, joined community groups, and sought out opportunities to connect with other immigrants. Slowly but surely, we began to adapt to the new surroundings and discovered a rich mosaic of Edmontonian heritage with cultures from all around the world. We learned to appreciate the beauty of Edmontonian winters, the kindness of strangers, and the vast opportunities that the city offered, especially to my child who was soon turning thirteen.

We visited the town of Banff and saw the Rockies right in front of us. There was a long pedestrian area, with streets filled with restaurants and cafes, no cars rushing by, just people casually walking up and down the streets with Beaver's Tail bread in hand or simply basking in the sun. It was a big contrast to the mountainous town of our homeland where Mount Everest Himalayan range can only be viewed from a distance. First of all, it is at an extremely high altitude and is almost uninhabitable, and secondly, there is no road access, there is no way to reach the mountains unless one treks for weeks with mountain gears and guides. There are no café-lined streets, instead we hear the striking sounds of bells hung around the neck of the mountain yaks, common in sparsely populated mountain villages where the yak herders live.

This contrasting infrastructure, in almost similar geographical landscape and temperatures, is very striking to me. I really appreciate the Canadian engineers and road builders who took time, and effort to make the town of Banff so beautiful. It is beyond my imagination, how people must have toiled with basic minimum technology and equipment and still build such a modern infrastructure design and layout.

Just as we were beginning to settle in our new life, the world was thrown into chaos by the COVID-19 pandemic. Border closures and travel restrictions separated our family as my husband could not be in Edmonton. My daughter and I had to face the challenges of a new city alone. The weight of loneliness and uncertainty was heavy on my shoulders. Video calls, though comforting, could not replace the warmth of being together, and sharing the experiences of everyday life.

The pandemic heightened our isolation. Social gatherings, even visits with friends were limited. Community events were canceled, and the once bustling city streets were eerily quiet. We found ourselves confined to the basement apartment we had rented at a friend's house. It seemed like the world had stopped to heal and to put our dreams on hold. The pandemic, with its constant threat of illness and uncertainty, added an extra layer of stress to the already challenging situation we faced.

In Winter, each snowflake that danced outside our window was a tiny reminder of the vast distance between me and my hot homeland. I had never experienced such a vast amount of snowfall in front of my house. It was a new experience to see this, to go out and walk in boots heavy with snow or make a snowman with my muffler wrapped around it. I felt cold, not just from the weather but from a deeper chill, the biting wind, and the unfamiliar silence of the house combined to create a perfect storm of loneliness. Yet, as I wrapped myself in a warm blanket and sipped on a cup of hot chocolate, a flicker of hope ignited within me. I remembered the kindness of neighbors, the warmth of the people at the community center, and the promise of a brighter future for my daughter. With renewed determination, I stepped up, ready to embrace the winter wonderland.

## The Power of Community Involvement

I settle on a daily routine as a way to cope. I wake up early, prepare breakfast for my daughter and get her ready for school. I then quickly get ready for work, ensuring I have all the documents and materials I need. I faced the challenges of public transportation, traffic congestion, and unpredictable weather. At work, I navigate through a new work culture, adapt to different work schedules, and strive to prove myself in a new environment. After work, I rush to the food bank to volunteer, sort food items, pack boxes, and interact with people from diverse backgrounds. In the evenings, I make sure to spend quality time with my daughter. Help her with homework, prepare dinner, watch movies late into the weekend nights and engage in fun activities. I often stay up late into the night to catch up, study for certifications, or simply to unwind.

As I watch my daughter who is engrossed in her school assignments, but occasionally glancing up at me with worried eyes, I realize I miss sitting with my mother, sipping freshly brewed home-garden tea and eating home-grown corn. I remember the smell of Rhododendron and Orchids, the dogs barking at a distance or children screaming in playgrounds. In quiet and worrying times, I unknowingly reach home in my mind. As a notification from my phone alerted me to a volunteer shift the next day at the food bank, I sigh as I realize the weight of my responsibilities. How can I do it all? As I drift off to sleep and reflect on the day, I feel a sense of accomplishment for balancing my various roles, but I'm exhausted. I wonder if I can keep up this pace and if it really is the right choice for my daughter and me.

Through my volunteer work at the Food Bank, I discovered a newfound sense of purpose. I am mesmerized by the diverse tapestry of cultures woven into the fabric of my work environment and the community I serve. The gratitude shining in the eyes of those I help fills me with a profound sense of satisfaction and accomplishment. I realize that I can make a positive impact on my community, even as a newcomer. I am charmed by Edmonton's rich heritage which inspires me to embrace its vibrant spirit. By connecting with other immigrants, I begin to build a network of friends and supporters. Sharing stories, laughter, and cultural experiences help me feel less isolated and more connected to my new home. I discover a sense of belonging, a place where I am valued and appreciated.

As I continue to volunteer, I find that helping others is a powerful way to heal. By focusing on the needs of others, I am able to temporarily forget my own worries and anxieties. The gratitude and appreciation I received from those I help truly fills me with a sense of purpose and meaning. Through my volunteer work, I also develop valuable skills and knowledge like how to organize events, manage budgets, improve communication skills, and work effectively with diverse groups of people. These skills not only benefit the community but also empower me to pursue my own goals and aspirations. As I help others, I am helping myself to grow and evolve.

While I sort through the donated food items, a sense of satisfaction washes over me. I am making a difference, no matter how small. One day, a child approaches me, shyly asking for help to get a toy. I smile and then patiently guide the child and give him a small red airplane toy. As the child's face lights up with joy and gratitude, my heart feels broader with the joy we then share together. At that moment, I found a place in this new world.

## A New Beginning

When the world started to recover from COVID, travel restrictions began to ease. After years of separation, my husband was finally able to be together with us. The joy and relief we felt was overwhelming, we hugged and cried and took photos to capture the moment.

Even though we are now reunited and happy, our family faces new challenges. Finding affordable housing in a competitive market proves difficult. The high cost of living puts a strain on our limited budget. Finding jobs that match our qualifications and experience was another hurdle, as both of us maneuver through a complex job market and unfamiliar workplace culture. Our daughter, meanwhile, is enjoying her school years at Hilwie Hamdon Junior High School, making new friends and taking part in new school activities.

Despite the obstacles, we are determined to remain resilient and seek assistance from the organizations that offer support to newcomers - attending workshops on job-seeking skills, resume writing, financial literacy, and job fairs. We also explore the options of part-time jobs and volunteer opportunities to gain experience and build networks. This added stress, at times, makes our home environment tense and not easy to cope with. Small victories, like finding affordable housing or securing a part time job becomes an occasion to celebrate.

With time, we integrate into the community and find fulfilling careers that allow us to contribute and think of buying a new home. I continue to volunteer, giving the little time I can manage to help others, and pay forward the kindness I once received, when I needed it the most. We are filled with gratitude for the opportunities and challenges that have shaped our lives. We also cannot forget the support we received from the community, employers, and new friends.

### Finding Home: An Inspiration to Fellow Immigrants

My story is a testament to the power of human resilience. My journey, marked by challenges such as cultural adjustment, language barriers, and separation from home, is a touching example of overcoming adversity and becoming stronger.

This also shows that a community is more than just a geographical location - it is a network of relationships that provide support, love, and a sense of belonging. It is accepting each other's strengths and weaknesses and honouring different heritages. For immigrants like me, community plays a crucial role in navigating the challenges of a new place through shared experiences, mutual support, cultural exchange, inspiring motivation and hope. Community helps preserve cultural traditions and values, providing a sense of identity and belonging.

Resilience allows us to transform adversity into opportunity. Not only are we overcoming challenges but also thriving in our new environment. Looking back, I feel a sense of gratitude and accomplishment. I've overcome countless challenges, built a strong community support system, and found happiness in my new home.

I am the strong independent person I am today because of the struggles I've overcome. I am  no longer just an immigrant; I am a Canadian, a mother, a friend, and an ardent believer in building strong communities.

# In praise of Edmonton Transit Services

**By Dan Li**

There is a country full of love and hope,
It is Canada, east of the Pacific Ocean.
There is a city that brings love and hope,
It is Edmonton, in north Alberta.

Who played this movement of love?
Who spread the light of hope?
It is Edmonton Transit Services,
It is the bus driver, the train operator, sitting in a small
    operating cabin.

I lost my wallet but it is back in my hand,
I cannot help but ask:
"How is the bus also a safe deposit box?"

When I look out of the bus shelter,
The driver stops his bus
"Are you all right? What can I do for you?"
When my eyes retreat from panic,
A shy smile softens the driver's face.
I cannot help thinking in my heart,
"He is not my family; how can he have their kind heart?"
"He is not my family; how can he have their warm smile?"

With the first ray of morning light,
Not shining on my window yet,
The bus already starts moving,
No matter how many people,

Randy Stennes, "DATS"

No matter how dark the skin or how white the face,
The bus goes on with its trip.
Even if there is no one on the seat,
The bus keeps going.
Knowing that someone is looking for it at the next stop.

The snow from the Rocky Mountains cannot block the train
    from running,
The winding roads of the city cannot stop the bus from
    running,
There is only one voice echoing in their ears:
"Depart on time, arrive on time!"

It has been bouncing along our city streets for 116 years,
Covering distance to circle the earth for many, many times.
From morning to night, from night to the morning light,
Year after year, it is always present.

When the spring rain fills the pond
And summer flowers show off their colorful garments
When maple leaves paint the mountains red
And the white snow covers the square
The bus never stops.
It is a greenhouse in winter
A cool cabin in summer.

The buses move with the shifts in Edmonton's history,
The drivers witness great changes and glories of our city.

During Covid-19, I hid at home,
The transit services still worked as usual.
It showed me, "Don't panic, everything is working normally,"
Conveyed love, comfort, and hope.

You may have no money, but you must have hope,
You may have no friends, but you must see the dawn.

How far and long can you walk?
The bus in Edmonton can replace your feet,
And accompany you all around the city.
Leave your car in the garage.
Help protect the environment,
Taking the public bus reduces carbon emissions.

ETS driving is an employment option for new immigrants.
Short-term professional training, long-term job security.
You won't need too much clothing,
Just wear a uniform to work every day.

Late nights
While I am asleep in my bed.
The buses are still busy on the road,
In the darkness the bus brings light,
And brings people safely home.

Early morning,
When little birds are not up yet to sing.
The bus is already on the road.
It is the bus that takes me to the classroom, to my workplace;
It is the bus that takes me to the mall, to the airport.
It gives me wings to fly,
It gives me hope,
It helps me realize my dreams.

Edmonton Transit Services
It connects my life and dreams,
It connects my life and hope.
It's a life experience I cannot forget.

Jamie Laventure, "Fort Ed"

# Old Bus Stop

**By William Wang**

Driving between the lines of day and night,
My bus engine sounds mechanically correct.
Passing the corner where you reside,
The old bus station is on the far side.

You turn away from my headlights,
Fumbling in your purse to find a cigarette,
Are you waiting for a ride?
Are you working tonight?

Cold skies and frostbites,
Unclear weather forecasts,
Should you turn left?
Should you turn right?

The seasons pass you by,
Is there a destination to decide?
Late buses starting to run citywide,
The sun will rise after twilight.

# A Stranger

**By William Wang**

Are you running late?
Am I arriving early?
You are nowhere in sight,
Perhaps my timing is not right.

Are you a stranger passing by?
Are you a regular catching this ride?
Do you need a moment to rest and sigh?
You seem a bit preoccupied.

A sheltering bus in which you can reside,
Lingering around for a longer ride,
With a worn-out backpack by your side,
Are you rerouting your path for a surprise?
Your hair is covering the corners of your weary eyes.

Chasing the sunset to West Ed,
Returning under the moonlight,
You said to me, "A meteor shower is best seen after midnight."
Suddenly, you lit up my sky.

Eli Abada, "Fish" Acrylic and coloured pencil 2024

# Interwoven

## By Khrystyna Zalutska

MY VERY BEING WAS PASSED ON TO ME.

The way I talk, the way I walk, and even the way I smile reflects all those who came before me. It is the same for everyone–we are never truly individual. Our thoughts, actions, and beliefs are motivated at least in some way by others. We are strung together by a ribbon embroidered with all our experiences. We are many colours intertwined to make one solid belief, thought, or voice.

I remember the warmth of my city. Ivano-Frankivsk was a charming place, with intricate buildings and artwork carefully placed throughout the streets—it filled me with wonder. I would run past the fountains, through flocks of pigeons, laughing as their wings fluttered wildly around me before they disappeared into the sky. Voices filled the air with constant chatter; everyone had something to say. All this brought me up, raised me, shaped my being, to be as I was then.

For a long time, I thought that I would not be complete because I left the people who were shaping me. My family and everyone else... they made me. How could I possibly let them go? At seven years old, I was told to say my goodbyes, and shortly after, Mama and I were on a plane.

For a time after we arrived in Edmonton, I lived in my memories. The present felt distant, almost unreal.

My Dido taught me to be kind and gentle, to always respect the world around me. He sang me songs that would forever stay in my heart and be swirled into the world around me. They made my world shine brighter.

My Baba always showed me how to be strong and brave. She taught me the monsters in my closet were not real; they existed only because I had to learn to overcome fear. She always told me that strength can take many different shapes. That was how we kept our heads up.

My Mama made me believe that my dreams were possibilities and not just thoughts in my head. She would say that as long as I put in the work, I would have an outcome that would make me happy. She would remind me of the whole "shoot for the moon; land among the stars" saying. She pushed me to go farther than I had ever thought I could go on my own. She showed me magic in the real world—taking me to the theatre, where we would sit together, eyes wide at the wonders unfolding on stage. I would gasp at the sights and clap until my hands were raw. I did not mind. I was happy.

My Tato was not always there, but when he was, he opened my eyes to the world, to the beauty in differences, the way they shone and created something extraordinary. He knew so much about so many places and people; about how other societies function. He helped me understand things at seven years old that some people never grasp in a lifetime.

And then I left my pretty city of Ivano-Frankivsk, and it felt like the songs were ripped from my heart. The world no longer shone, and the monsters began crawling out of my closet every night. The magic faded, leaving me cold. Always cold. When

I left, the ribbon that bound me was replaced with some clear tape and band-aids to haphazardly keep it together. I saw for myself all the different things in the world that my dad talked about. In this way, I was prepared to leave.

There were no more beautiful cities and painstakingly detailed streets; instead, I was left with beige and grey blocks for buildings, with a weird smell I could never quite place. The snow always seemed dirty, and the sun made me feel sick with its closeness. Back home, the sky was vast, and I had room to breathe. But here, it was not the same. The sky taunted me, pressing down, almost as if it were in a continuous fall, screaming at me to hold it up—crushing me with its weight. I was so tired. But I could not be tired—the sky would crush me if I gave in.

Sometimes I remember how angry I got at the people around me. They could not understand me, and they did not bother trying. It was difficult to have no one to relate to. I think back to when my Tato would take me fishing—it was his way of cheering me up. He took me fishing a lot when I was younger. I would sit and watch him as the boat rocked gently on the waves. The fishing reel bobbed up and down, and I would chew on a pepperoni stick, unimpressed by the entire process. But then I would feel a sharp tug, drop my snack, and laugh as I reeled in the line, the fish fighting back. It would leap from the water, glistening in the sunlight before diving back in. My dad would cheer, his joy contagious, and he would film the moment on his phone, narrating my victory.

When I held up the fish for a picture, I felt like I belonged– I was with somebody who understood me. The water sparkled, birds sang, and for a brief moment, the magic returned through the beautiful nature all around me.

Slowly, I began to see the world around me again. I saw the warm smiles of my friends, the blessings of a culture still alive in me despite the distance from its origin. I found PLAST, the Ukrainian Youth Organization, where we spoke only Ukrainian while hiking through the Edmonton River Valley or sang carols at Christmas, spreading joy wherever we went. I studied my culture, history, literature, and much more at the Ivan Franko School of Ukrainian Studies in Edmonton. I did Ukrainian theatre here as well. My friends loved it, and I loved them. Slowly, the sun began to warm my face again. Tiny strings, formed from my new memories, floated all around me—not yet a ribbon, but strands that could one day weave into something intricate and beautiful.

I saw my community—the one where we danced, sang, and performed together. The one that taught me to love nature. The one that carried our history, literature, and language. These communities wrapped themselves around me, their threads weaving into my life, strengthening what had frayed.

Little by little, new threads wove into my ribbon. Every person I met, every laughter shared, every song sung, every memory made—they all became part of the fabric. The old fragments wrapped around them, binding them together into something whole again.

With every fish, every song, every performance, every laugh, the magic my mama spoke of began to return. I saw it in the trees as they swayed, in the streams as the water danced, and in the endless crowd of people navigating their paths through life. I felt it in the air—thick and alive. I saw it in the smiles of strangers, heard it in the laughter of children, and felt it in the warmth of the sun on my skin. I felt the monsters melt into puddles, and I felt myself being kind again.

Even on the coldest days, the sun still managed to shine so brightly. That was true magic.

# *awareness & insights*

Being an immigrant means carrying your homeland on your back, and still finding the strength to walk forward, while navigating new paths of language, culture, ideas, and trying to shape a future for yourself and often your family as well. It's a lot of learning, growth, and responsibility.

# The Turnaround

**By Emily Tworek**

My Dad's mother, whom I never call "Grandma," was born in Edmonton in 1933. Our family calls her Babci (pronounced bup-shee), in keeping with our Polish heritage. I didn't realize the importance of maintaining my heritage until I found myself in a job that tested my resolve every day. Whenever I found myself wanting to quit, stories of my Babci enabled me to keep moving forward.

She grew up in a time where even daily life could test her resolve. Her positive perspective is a special thing that I don't believe can be inherited. But learning it is possible, and a day came when I was grateful that I did.

*When Babci was young, her father got a job on the CNR railroad and moved the whole family out to Hargwen, which was then just two houses and a station – it could hardly be called a town. Her parents only spoke Ukrainian at home. When Babci went to school, she could not understand the lessons until a friend taught her English. Post -graduation, Babci and the other girls only had three career options: nurse, secretary, or teacher. Babci and friends mulled over their limited choices and decided on Nursing. I do not think Babci ever looked back after making that decision. When she showed me an old picture of herself in a nurse's uniform, she had the most radiant smile.*

Two generations later, despite all the options available to me, I did not feel the same confidence about my life decisions. How could Babci have found success, yet I had almost unlimited choices and still struggled?

It took me two degrees to find out what I wanted to do. I completed four years of Engineering and two years of work before having a "quarter-life crisis." It was then that I went back to school for another degree, this time in Animation. The pandemic hit during my first year of my second degree.

Maybe it was some of Babci's perseverance, but I made it through the following three years, making ends meet through government assistance and a part-time job at an online educational company. At the end of my third year, I was laid off from my part-time job. I faced a wide-open summer of semi-lockdown, no job, and fading relationships with my friends because of a long isolation. I could have considered myself lucky for being a student during this tough time. But all I could think was how behind in life I felt.

Short on options and in need of cash, I accepted an unlikely job that a friend suggested I fill: auditing work crews at a petrochemical plant near my city of Red Deer. *At least it will be a short commute*, I thought begrudgingly. After I accepted the job, I discovered it would actually be at the other operation site near Edmonton.

I thought about rescinding my acceptance. Making the move to Edmonton hardly seemed worth it for a six-week gig. Wouldn't it be easier to find something closer to home? The contracting company sent me instructions to go to a supplier in Red Deer and pick up a set of coveralls for myself and a coworker. I sat in my car with the coveralls, still thinking about cancelling the contract. I unfolded one set. They already had my name stitched onto them: *Emily Tworek.*

*The name Tworek is Polish and draws to mind my industrious immigrant relatives: doctors and business owners who settled in the city of Edmonton after fleeing brutal post-war conditions. Babci took the name when she married my grandfather in 1956, while he was still in medical school. After years of moving around for his work, they finally settled into a home in Saint Albert, where they lived for 17 years. When my grandfather grew tired of doing surgery, he sought meaningful volunteer work that matched his skills. After some inquiring, he got a letter from the Holy Rosary Sisters of Ireland. They needed a volunteer to assist at their hospital in Anyigba, Nigeria. It was a two-year commitment, so my grandparents would have to sell their home if they wanted to go. I am sure they had apprehensions, but that did not change their minds. They made their arrangements and set off.*

For reasons I could not explain, I decided to go ahead with the job. My sister living in Edmonton offered me a spare room in her apartment, so I arranged to move in with her for the next six weeks.

I arrived early on my first day, after commuting an hour from Edmonton to the plant. My new coworker, Ned, was already waiting outside the training centre. He was an older, scruffy looking man who looked as tired as I felt. He took the coveralls I handed him and muttered something like *thank you*. After a brief rundown of site protocols in the training centre, we returned to the parking lot for our ride. Ned wandered off while I sat there, miserably calculating how many shifts I would be stuck doing. Our ride showed up a few minutes later. She was a young, spunky woman named Jen. We stopped by the second-floor office to pick up the personal protective equipment (PPE) we would need to walk around the site. Covid protocols were in effect, so all of us were masked. I tried on safety goggles, my breath fogging them up. I also received a hardhat, gloves, and hearing protection. We decided to take the elevator back down. As we were getting in the elevator, Jen told us all to face the wall. "Covid protocol" she explained.

She showed us to our "office": one of a lengthy line of trailers set up for the contracting crews. Inside the trailer, a single row of desks was lined up along the far wall, each desk separated from the other by plastic curtains. On the opposite wall was a charging station for our radios, some coat hooks, and a small drink station. Some of the desks were already occupied by people in coveralls working on digital tablets. Jen showed me to my desk and handed me a tablet. I hardly had time to get my boots on before we were heading out to the van that would drop us off near the work crews we would audit. After some introductions, there was a small amount of amiable chatter in the van. Ned, however, rode in solemn silence.

We stopped where the work crews were mustering. They were divided by their profession: pipefitters, scaffolders, welders, etc. Jen told me I would be with the scaffolders. She introduced me to them, giving a short speech about our role. We went by a title that I can no longer remember - something to avoid using the word "auditor": We were there on behalf of the plant owner to watch the contracting crews work and keep track of "inefficiencies." None of the scaffolders looked happy to see us. That day, they would be building a structure for some repairs taking place on second level piping in the ethylene unit. We followed them as they carried supplies out to the job site. As the crew got to work setting up, Jen told me to pick a crew member at random, record each of their activities, and assign each activity to a category such as "on task," "on break," or "planned meeting."

Jen spent a few minutes watching what I put down before she deemed my assessments acceptable and left to check on someone else. After she left, I stood there, acutely aware of how I was watching them and how maddening it would feel to *be* watched. I tried to make myself invisible. Sometimes, it was difficult to decide a category for the task. Crew members often stopped to talk. How long before a quick chat became an "unplanned break" and then counted as off-task? Sometimes the crewmate I was watching would disappear into the maze of scaffolding and I would have to follow him, getting awkwardly close.

The day passed agonizingly slowly. Taking my boots off in the trailer at shift-end, I heard Ned yelling at Jen over something petty. I left as soon as I could.

I arrived at work the next day to find out that Ned had been fired. He had a bad attitude to be sure, but I could not shake the realization of just how expendable we were as contractors. Every day I met a new crew, each less excited to see me than the next. To top it off, that summer was aggressively hot, a rare heat dome trapping the sun's rays near ground level. The temperature rose to around 40C at the hottest point of the day. We sweated in the stagnant air under our full PPE and face masks.

*Babci told me that in Anyigba people spent their time indoors having a siesta during the hottest point of the day. There was only electricity in the morning and a little in the evening. She had to boil and filter the water before she could drink it or use it to wash vegetables. Babci said it was not so bad though, growing up in the 1930's she had learned to accept that everyday tasks were tough sometimes. She did all her cooking in the morning hours. She told me she was incredibly grateful to have had running water for showers. The volunteer allowance she and my grandfather had was small but enough. They appreciated all the people they met, including the kind Sisters who worked at the hospital.*

Sometimes I was paired up with another auditor for a day. My coworkers were nice people and chatting with them provided a welcome distraction from the heat. As the summer wore on however, relations between co-workers began to sour. One of our team-mates, Brad, who had previously seemed laid back, began to insist on managing our shifts and supervising our work. Dan, a large, loud-mouthed man, exhibited similar controlling behaviour, despite being no further up the ranks than we were. My coworker's reliability began to drop due to various circumstances, and they took sick days or showed up late more often. Some ended up getting fired. Others took the job too seriously, even following crew members on their bathroom breaks, leading to altercations and harassment.

I sat at the desk next to Dan. I tried to keep my head down and pretended to laugh at his mean-spirited jokes. When he badmouthed me, I would snap back as casually as I could, which only made him laugh more.

The site turnaround started near the end of summer. During this time, equipment was shut down for maintenance. Every second of equipment shutdown was a dollar lost for the plant owner. So everyone needed to work overtime and around the clock until the shutdown was complete. The crew shifts increased from 10 hours to 12 hours, 6 days a week, and our schedules followed suit.

The mood in the trailer was less than jovial. Those who were fired had not been replaced. We split into day and night shifts. Our resources spread thin, we would no longer be able to work in pairs. I had hoped that Jen would be staying with those of us on day shift, but we got Dan instead. His yelling only got worse under the stress. All of us were exhausted and short-tempered.

The results of our observations were not encouraging either. Despite the small leeways we gave to work crews, we had still been reporting high rates of inefficiencies (by the plant owner's standards). The plant owner did not care for this, and wanted to crack down even further by having us take down individual badge numbers of underperforming crew members for potential follow-up. I had been fine with recording things anonymously. But this was going too far. I did not want to be responsible for getting anyone in trouble, knowing how easily contractors were let go. I tried to shake this feeling and just follow orders, but I could not. I was grateful for the small positive moments I had managed to have with crew members, jokes or stories shared that had made the work more bearable. Being responsible for ratting them out was too much for me to stomach.

When I brought my misgivings forward to my team, it did not sit well with Dan. He told me I needed to follow this order and that was the end of it.

"I won't do it." I said, surprising myself.

One of the Site supervisors from the plant happened to be in the trailer, chatting with Jen, who was just getting off her shift.

"Let's see what *he* thinks about this." said Dan, smirking as he went to fetch him.

I stood there frozen, thinking this was it. I would get fired. I pictured packing up and going home. My heart sank.

Dan brought the Site Supervisor over and said, "She won't take badge numbers down."

"Is this true?" asked the Site Supervisor.

"It just doesn't feel right," I answered.

To my surprise, the Site Supervisor agreed that this was an unreasonable thing to ask. He actually seemed glad I had said something. Relieved, I tried not to look at Dan, who was barely containing his outrage. In truth, everyone had had enough of Dan's controlling attitude and anger issues. A few days later, I returned to the trailer at the end of a long shift to find Dan's desk empty. I walked back to my car in the sunset light, feeling a weight lifted.

*Babci told me that when night fell in Anyiga, and the burning sun vanished, the sky felt soft, like it was a different sky entirely.*

After Dan left, the air itself seemed to cool. I kept at my work, even feeling grateful at times for my exhaustion at the end of the day, which allowed me to collapse into a restful sleep night after night. I gradually got better at warming the work crews up to me, usually by making a self-deprecating joke about auditing. I tried to make my sympathy for their frustrations clear. To be useful, I helped gather supplies when they needed

One way to tell which auditors were on the good side of the work crews was by looking at their hardhats. Most of the crews had company stickers among their stationary supplies. If you built a rapport with them, sometimes they would give you one to put on your hard hat. I collected so many that my hard hat was covered.

Shortly before my contract was set to end, I was sitting in the lunchroom, idly wondering how I'd made it through. Did my heritage endow me with extra resilience? I didn't think so. As I'd learned in the past six weeks, heritage is more than just who your ancestors are. It's learning how they see the world through the stories they pass along. I'd like to think that if Babci worked this same job, her hardhat would be covered too.

I checked my email before heading back to work. To my surprise I found a message from my old boss, asking me to come back now that Covid was over. I gladly accepted and headed to my sister's with the good news. A few weeks later, I left Edmonton for Red Deer, dirty boots and coveralls in the trunk, and my hardhat resting in the passenger seat.

**Jamie Laventure,**
**"Bluejay"**
**Monoprint**
(Opposite page)

# Getting My Hands Dirty
# in My New Home

By Mila Bongco-Philipzig

IN THE EARLY 2000s, JUST BARELY A YEAR AFTER MY FAMILY AND I arrived in Edmonton, I rented a plot at a community garden along 104 avenue and east of 109 street. The previous summer, late August, I had stumbled upon this garden when it was blooming profusely, bursting with precious abundance. There was a mixture of shrubs, trees, flowers, and vegetables, but mostly vegetable patches of greens, spilling out in complete disorder, covering some pathways with leaves, some almost a foot wide. It was not a pristine garden with well-maintained pathways, and well-trimmed shrubs, and plants growing in rows – oh no! It was the wildness and the lushness of the garden that called out to me. The garden on a stretch of street blocks was surrounded by glass and concrete of university buildings. Situated along a busy avenue, this patch of colourful, bountiful life stood out and reminded me how I have not gardened in years, have not been immersed in nature, and have lost my connection to land. So, I inquired how to join, and luckily, was granted a plot for the next year.

Early the next Spring, my five-year-old son and I went to the plot assigned to us. It must be pretty common knowledge in Edmonton that a garden looks very different in Spring than when it is in full bloom during Summer. But I did not come from a country with four seasons, so what I saw was a shock to me. In the tropics, the trees and shrubs never totally lose their leaves, and there is always greenery on the land. So, I was expecting a pared down version of the garden I saw last summer, not a cold, desolate looking almost bare stretch of land, with patches of snow and lots of mud, some dry and empty branches and knotty twigs stretching from shrubs and trees. The shed, which looked quaint and charming behind vines, flowers, and full trees last summer was now fully exposed and looked run down. It was still locked. I picked up a fairly big stick and struck the ground to test the soil. The stick snapped, and I slipped and almost fell. I could not believe how hard the ground was. How can anything grow here? I wondered. How will I dig? How can I plant anything? Maybe I just won't garden after all, I thought.

Suddenly, I heard my son shout "Mom! Look!"

I looked up to where he was pointing and saw what must be hundreds of birds, all flying together as one, swirling and swooping, twisting and turning together in ever-changing patterns. My son and I watched in silence, mesmerized. I learned later they were starlings.

"This place is cool," my son said as the birds flew further away.

"It's not this place," I retorted, "you can see that anywhere."

"No, we never see things like that in our apartment," my son said, still looking up at the now empty sky.

He was right. We had been cooped up in our apartment. What no one tells you when you decide to immigrate, is that prior to leaving your homeland, you will spend many years searching for documents, filling out forms, running after appointments, paying fee after fee after fee. Then, when you get to the new place, you will be beleaguered with the same things: documents, forms, fees, appointments.

My son's comments made me decide to pursue community gardening. I thought it would be a good reason to make us stay outside and connect more with nature.

Over that summer, I learned a lot about gardening in Zone 3 (in comparison to gardening in the Philippines which is in Zone 14). But more than that, I learned a lot about Edmonton, about my neighbours, about the assumptions, experiences, and knowledge we bring as immigrants that could impact our settling into a new place, a new home.

Community gardening can be daunting for a new immigrant without a vehicle. Even if there were shared tools and equipment available, one still had to bring a lot for one's own use. The other gardeners helped me a lot. Most of them were elderly ladies. Then there was Diane who was younger and stronger, and she showed me how to till through the stubborn, stodgy clay in one part of our plot and showed me how to manage the drainage. She bought bags of peat moss and fertilizer for me, and the other gardeners shared their compost. They taught me how to read plant packets, what to plant with each other, when best to plant and how to take care of my plot. They told me how to check the weather daily and what to do when there was too much heat, how to check and what to do for bugs and slugs and blights. I would not have learned any of this without all these people taking the time to talk to me. Internet? Cell phone? They were not as ubiquitous then. As a reference, it was only in 2002 that the first Blackberry was released, about the same time wireless networks improved technology to allow the shift to smartphones.

My son had the run of the place, and he was very happy being dirty – digging with his own trowels, playing with bugs, sloshing water around, using branches as swords. He got cookies from everybody, and Maureen, the garden director, made him in charge of the strawberry patch. She taught him how to put straws under the fruit, what to do with the shoots, and best of all, showed us how to pick ripe berries while still warm from the sun and pop them into our mouths.

The community garden gave us good reasons to be outdoors. We also managed to explore our neighborhood more as we took different walking paths, and this enriched our experiences of settling down and our sense of belonging in Edmonton. I could talk to people at work about gardening and my growing knowledge of Edmonton.

At harvest time, many of the older gardeners needed help harvesting, so Diane and I obliged. My son helped, too, putting the vegetables into buckets. Diane packed much of the harvest into containers and loaded them into her truck. She said they usually donate the extra harvest to two places: Meals on Wheels and The Marian Centre. She asked for help loading and unloading the containers. This was good exposure for me since until then I didn't even know that one could donate fresh produce to centers.

When I asked Maureen if I could keep my plot for the next year, I was devastated to hear that the community garden at this location will be shut down. Grant MacEwan University was expanding and needed the area for more buildings and parking lots. I never saw the people I met at that community garden again, and I never even got the chance to say good-bye. Not even Diane. But they gave me so much care and knowledge that still nourish me to this day.

Not long after, we were able to buy our first home in the Hazeldean neighborhood, an old area with small houses in big lots, surrounded by numerous big, mature trees. I was happy to find a well-tended vegetable garden at the back of the house, the soil was well-fertilized, and the area was bright and sunny. I gardened there happily for about five years, some years better than others. Each year, I made sure I planted extra rows to donate to Meals on Wheels, The Marian Centre, or Edmonton's Food Bank. Unfortunately, I lost most of the sunny spots on my vegetable garden and my prime gardening area became much smaller when a huge duplex rose beside our house after our neighbor sold their lot. In 2009, the City of Edmonton announced its Infill Housing project. Hazeldean and the surrounding areas started redevelopment with lot splitting for Infill houses, and most of these were tall, skinny homes or big multiple dwellings replacing the original bungalows. We lost many big, mature trees in the process, and it was only in 2021 that a public tree protection bylaw was put in place for the city. There are still no laws regulating tree removal on private property.

Every year, when I prepare my garden, I feel some sadness and loss as I remember my community garden replaced by a parking lot, as I notice my smaller gardening space, as I see more buildings rise up and more and more trees and open space disappear. But I keep gardening because planting always makes me happy and hopeful. Planting opens up opportunities to tend something beautiful and nourishing. I now view Spring as possibilities for fresh, new starts. "To plant a garden means to believe in tomorrow," as Audrey Hepburn once said.

I always garden with bare hands. I like the feel of soil between my fingers. It makes me feel connected to nature and makes me feel I am doing something to take care of my new home, in this new land. I feel the land has been very giving and forgiving, allowing me to harvest root crops even on those years I had not been steady in watering and weeding.

"This is home now," I tell myself whenever I touch Canadian soil.

The sense of home is a complex, ever-changing concept for immigrants as we stay connected to both our old and new cultures, as we grapple with holding on to our memories while building a future in a new place. Gardening – working with the land, coaxing life from the land – has helped me feel more grounded in my new home. I feel joy and gratitude in taking care of this land, just as it has been taking care of me.

AMYNA/4
O.IRAN,4

# SAAN PA?

**By Candice Joy Oliva**

The email comes mid-December
My heart drops with the tap of my finger
A loss we expected, knocked on our door
To tell us it's been inside all along
Our so-promised final garden season
A joy anticipated, has just left
Taking the dinner table with them
Where will we gather now?

Tell me, *where else* will we go?

SAAN PA magpapasalamat for an endless pot of soup made
   from vegetables harvested here?
SAAN PA masusubukan ang tibs with injera after planting
   rows and rows of seeds?
SAAN PA maaalok ang mga kaibigan to bury peas and
   cucumbers as companions to tell them I'm glad we were
   planted together too?
SAAN PA tayo makikibahagi sa mga kuwento't kultura ng
   ating kapwa?
SAAN PA dadapo ang paroparo when we honor the land and
   cleanse ourselves with smoke?
SAAN PA aabraso under the crabapple tree waiting for your
   turn of bánh xèo?
SAAN PA aabang ng samosas from the Punjab Parantha Hut
   after hilling potatoes after potatoes?

**Amynah Pirani, "Flowers"**
**Waterolour 2024**
(Opposite page)

SAAN PA tatakbo next door in the June rain for some fishball and kwek kwek after work?

SAAN PA tayo tuturo't matututo ng iba't ibang wika't pagbati sa isa't isa?

SAAN PA dadaloy ang musika ni Sebastian Barrera while we pull weed after weed, before pulling each other up and around to baile?

SAAN PA makikinig sa 月亮代表我的心 while the moon and us dance against the blue sky?

SAAN PA malalaman how borage, nasturtium or squash flowers taste on a birthday cake?

SAAN PA makakapaghandog ng iba't ibang prutas, gulay at halaman just to watch faces and smiles light up?

SAAN *NA* tayo gagala?

SAAN *NA* tayo lilibang?

SAAN *NA* tayo tatambay?

# UMA

**By Candice Joy Oliva**

For three years, I have worked in the Urban Farm.

*Hardin* doesn't quite fit, it's more than a community garden
It's not *bukid*, not amongst the hurried sprawl of the city
The closest thing I would call it in my language is UMA—
Like my grandparents' farm where I used to run wild outside

Picking calamansi under the sun for a later joy
Then watching pili nuts nearly dry out my patience
Before a pitying adult finally takes out a hammer to break one
Offering me the creamy nutty kernel of heaven inside the shell.

In conjuring UMA from my Bikol region, I honor that for many
    of us
This land is an echo of another country, another farm, another
    community
We come here to keep that memory alive for us, for the next
    generation.

On this blind and lively corner of 113 Avenue & 79 Street,
Tucked between gravel and chain link, elm and yarrow
Follow the maze of bees and butterflies to two acres of UMA
Where tobacco, sweet grass or cedar greets you as you enter

Where 20-some groups garden, grow and learn together
Red barn easily missed by festival goers, sports fans and dog
    walkers
Fondly, we think it's a very Edmonton trait: to be a hidden
    gem.

They said it used to be a lettuce farm, a sunflower field
And before that, it was all leftovers of concrete foundation
They kept digging up little reminders of the life UMA had—
11 years filling a museum frame with keys, needles and tiles.

They told me about the rototillers it took to break the
    driveways
About the pile of garbage, they turned into a compost hill
Of the soil they raised brimming with life & death
How it has given us years of harvest & abundance.

My family moved to Edmonton 11 years ago too;
Soon, UMA will become houses again.

No one knows seasons & cycles better than us gardeners
But we also know our perennials & annuals deeply
We think of the walking onion, the mint migrating to the path
We think of the sunflowers and amaranth past the iron fence

And maybe, we'll be alright.

Our faith in our ecosystem of roots
And seeds treasured over the years
will take us to new places to call UMA.

# UGMA

**By Candice Joy Oliva**

Unbidden, it comes—
A shriek of delight disrupts my dilemma
Of whether to stay for a while longer or go home.

If a chick could giggle and pitter patter with glee,
Then my eyes could not be deceiving me.
We have a runner from the coop!

A track-and-fly star dodging pits, palms and pockets,
Soaring through any thrown cloth or basket.
I pull out my phone to record our laughter.

I was once like that too,
Adventure-bright eyes set on a new city.
Game, set, play. Try and catch me!

# Seeking Happiness in Edmonton: A Journey of Self-Discovery

By Ying Shi

## A New Beginning

THE FIRST DAY I ARRIVED IN CANADA AS AN IMMIGRANT, I WAS FULL of dreams. I just came from China, where I ran an English school for ten years, and I was determined to continue my work in this new country. My plan was simple—build a bridge between my business in China and the opportunities here in Canada. I imagined myself creating something that merged the best aspects of both countries.

Over the next eight years, I dedicated myself to obtaining a Ph.D. in ESL (English as a Second Language) teacher education. I worked at three different universities and engaged in numerous research projects. It was like I was sowing seeds, longing for them to bear fruit, yet nothing seemed to take root. I felt like a loser trapped in a cycle of fruitless effort. After a sleepless night, full of anxiety, a realization dawned on me that would transform my life: *I was not cut out to work for others; I had to forge my own way.*

With newfound resolve, I resigned from my secure university job and decided to take a leap of faith to pursue my entrepreneurial dreams. The excitement was overwhelming. I signed up for a government-sponsored micro-business training program, set up my Sunshine English Education Company, and worked around the clock to create new courses, build a website, and recruit a small team of teachers. At first, it felt like the universe was opening to me—I built a brand, and I was finally getting the chance to do what I loved. Despite these promising beginnings, the company struggled to transform into a formal, self-sustaining operation.

A year and a half of solitary effort took its toll. The vibrant, bustling school life I had envisioned, filled with eager learners and dynamic energy, faded into a distant dream. I began to question myself. One particularly boring day, I had a startling thought: *Would anyone even be willing to hear me teach if I pay them $100?* The idea seemed so ridiculous, I almost laughed, but it only deepened my sense of hopelessness. I was at my lowest point, unsure whether I should continue or give up altogether.

In desperation, I turned to a former professor, a wise woman who had guided me through many of my academic struggles. She suggested that I apply for a position at a nonprofit immigrant English training program, LINC (Language Instruction for Newcomers to Canada), warning me that it was not an academic role and might not align with my grand aspirations. But like a drowning person; I needed something or anything to keep me afloat. So, I applied, hoping that it would at least get me out of isolation.

## The Interview

On the day of the interview, I felt a strange mixture of anxiety and excitement. I had never liked working in a nonprofit institution, but I was eager to seize any opportunity.

While navigating through three buses and the LRT (Light Rail Transit) system, my mind was racing with thoughts of how I had come to this point in my life. Finally, I arrived at the building—a low, nondescript structure nestled beside a football field. Its dull, faded walls did not inspire much hope.

As I approached the entrance, I saw a group of women in black robes and headscarves walking toward me. They moved slowly, almost deliberately, as though the world around them did not matter. Their presence made me feel small, and the unfamiliarity of their culture and clothing left me unsettled. The dimly lit corridor added to the sense of strangeness. My instincts screamed at me to turn around and leave, but my desperation of getting back to the outside world would not allow it. Instead, I steeled myself and knocked on the office door.

Not too surprising, I was hired. The assistant principal explained that the job was to teach basic English to help new immigrants adjust to Canadian life. Although it was not what I had trained for, I gratefully accepted, uncertain about what lay ahead.

## The Struggles

As soon as I started teaching, I was starkly reminded of how far I had strayed from my original grand aspirations. The school's facilities were old and outdated, and my students—many refugees from war-torn regions—came with traumatic personal histories. Some had never received formal education. My work shifted from guiding university students toward academic success to helping newcomers learn how to buy groceries, ride the bus, and fill out job applications in English. It was humbling and frustrating.

But the greatest challenge came from within me. No matter how hard I tried, I could not shake the feeling that I had failed since I had never stopped looking for academic jobs, and despite multiple applications and interviews, I could not land a position that matched my qualifications. My previous company was closed. My husband changed his mind about traveling around the world in early retirement, so I needed to keep working to stay at the same pace. When I tried to return to my former university, my previous director, though sympathetic, reminded me that they had already filled my position by one of over five hundred applicants worldwide.

One semester passed. Just as I was hesitating to stay, I was informed that my contract wouldn't be renewed due to low enrollments. I packed up my belongings and left unhappy and somewhat distressed.

During the summer, I launched another phase of job hunting, but once again, no offers came.

## A Moment of Truth

Two months went by.

Unexpectedly, the assistant principal from LINC reached out with an email offering a newly created position for me. Warmth and joy began to fill my heart. Though some of my students were still refugees with difficult pasts, I approached my work with growing gratitude.

One day, near the end of a Friday class, I suggested a lighthearted activity: "Let's share our happy childhood memories."

My students fell silent. After much encouragement, finally, a middle-aged woman raised her hand. "Teacher," she began hesitantly, "it's not that we don't want to participate. We just did not have happy childhoods."

I forced a smile. "That can't be true," I replied, my tone betraying disbelief.

The student said, "Teacher, if you don't mind, can I tell you an unhappy experience?"

"Of course you can!" It was a speaking practice anyway, and it did not matter what they would say.

She lifted her left sleeve, revealing an absent arm. "My brother-in-law shot it off," she said simply.

The atmosphere in the classroom instantly froze, and the temperature dropped to freezing point.

She looked down, seemingly void of emotion. "I was sick and hospitalized. A male villager stopped by to see me. We had a pleasant chat. It just so happened that my brother-in-law came in and saw me laughing, and he pulled out a gun and shot me. The arm couldn't be saved."

"Why would he do that?" a student asked, breaking the silence.

"Because I shouldn't have been alone with another man," she answered matter-of-factly.

For a moment, no one moved. The silence was deafening, the weight of her words suffocating.

And then another student spoke up. Her voice trembled as she shared her story. "I'm from a small village in Afghanistan. The Taliban raided our village and killed my parents. My brother and I had to run to the mountains. We ran and ran for what felt like forever, just to escape the chase."

I don't remember how the class ended. All I recall is rushing home and collapsing onto my bed, sobbing uncontrollably. The weight of their stories and their pain pressed down on me, and I could no longer hold back. The sobs were silent, but they came from the deepest part of me, as if every part of my soul were mourning—not just for them, but for the world that had allowed such suffering.

For the first time, I grieved not for myself, but for others. From that moment on, my students were no longer "them." They became *us*, and I became one of them.

## A New Path Forward

Everything changed.

It became important to me to convince my students that they were capable of learning, of soaring to heights they never imagined.

I started exploring their potential by introducing Gardner's multiple intelligence tests at the start of each semester, and the results amazed me. My students' cognitive abilities were as diverse and rich as those of the Canadian university students I had once taught in a different life. It was as if I had stumbled upon a hidden treasure trove of talent and promise.

Our lessons evolved into vibrant, hands-on task-based projects. I led my students to create healthy meal plans for their families in line with Canada's Food Guide. Driven by a new sense of responsibility, they delved deep into nutritional details, determined to ensure their family members had a balanced diet.

They presented in-depth research on local parks and historical sites, breathing life into the stories of the places they called home. And then there was the unforgettable visit to the Alberta Legislature building, where they came face-to-face with the MLA in charge of education. It was a moment that made their studies feel tangible, real.

We set aside time to explore and celebrate Indigenous culture. Our journey of discovery involved participating in National Indigenous Peoples Day events and conducting interviews at Edmonton City Hall. These experiences were not merely educational; they were eye-opening, expanding the students' perspectives significantly.

While studying the Alberta Employment Standards Code, the students formed groups to explore topics of interest: contracts, wages, overtime, vacations, benefits, among others. Each group actively researched, analyzed cases, and presented their findings creatively. Some performed skits, while others used power points for presentation. But the highlight was the class job fair. The students, dressed in their finest formal wear, their résumés carefully crafted and polished, stepped into a world of mock interviews. Booths set up by their peers awaited, and it was a test of their skills, a decisive moment.

In Edmonton's downtown-themed unit, the "classroom" expanded beyond the four walls of our campus. We ventured into the Edmonton Public Library where the students read and retold their favorite stories. We watched in awe as the Parade of the Edmonton Klondike Days Festival marched by, a spectacle of color and culture. Strolling through the North Saskatchewan River Valley, we soaked in the beauty of nature and the history that surrounded us. Back in class, the students' presentations were a testimony to their experiences, filled with newfound knowledge and deep reflections.

However, one experience stands out as the most unforgettable of all: the visit to the CBC Radio One Edmonton station. Once, as we entered, the veteran host Don Bell greeted us with a warmth that immediately put us at ease. His English stories on the "Learning English with CBC" platform were a goldmine for listening practice. The students were already familiar with his voice and stories.

And then there was Carol Amadeo, the morning news anchor. Every day at 10 a.m., her warm, rich voice filled our ears as she delivered the five-minute latest news segment about Edmonton, Alberta, Canada, and the world. The students listened intently, scribbling notes, and volunteers bravely shared the key stories in class. The students were always thrilled with the prospect of meeting her in person, and she often graciously stepped out of the studio to greet us, engaging in friendly chats.

All these visits were expertly organized and led by Chris Martin, the host and producer of a Saturday evening music show. A highlight was his mock interviews with some volunteers, during which he inspired the students to enhance their communication skills. A few times, Chris attended our class-end celebrations, where his presence and enjoyment of the potluck created a warm, big family atmosphere.

As I dedicated myself to teaching them real-life skills, preparing them for the challenges of work or further studies, and helping them dream of brighter, better futures, I felt a profound change within me.

Over time, in this new role, I did not just teach; I connected. I was not just a teacher anymore; I was their ally, their unwavering support. And with every passing day, every interaction, I realized that I had stumbled upon something truly precious. I had rediscovered my sense of purpose.

## The Presentation

Two years slipped away. One morning, as I prepared to leave for work, an unexpected realization hit me: I was happy. If my life ended that day, I would have had no regrets.

The transformation puzzled me at first. Reflecting on my journey, I remembered my workplace arranged for teachers to participate in a professional development conference where the keynote speaker introduced the theory of joyful education. Why shouldn't I apply this theory to my teaching?

In 2017, I submitted a proposal for a research-based presentation to the TESL (Teaching English as Second Language) Canada Conference held in the city of Niagara Falls, titled *A Journey of Discovering the Power of Joyful Learning*. The proposal was accepted, and my institution approved my attendance at the conference.

My presentation was scheduled for the final time slot on the last afternoon of the conference, a time when some attendees had already left to travel home. Presenters in that time slot were informed that their sessions might be canceled if attendance was too low.

When the time came, I walked into the designated room and took my place at the podium. Attendees began to take their seats, and by the time the session was about to start, every seat was filled. Soon, the back of the room was packed tightly with people standing.

With a smile, I told the story of how my students and I had redeemed each other, recounting my journey of seeking and discovering happiness in Edmonton.

When I finished and expressed my thankfulness, the room erupted in applause, and the audience suddenly rose to their feet. It was overwhelming. For the first time in years, I felt a deep sense of accomplishment. But more than that, I felt joy. Real joy.

## Epilogue

When the COVID - 19 pandemic hit, I faced a painful decision. The urge to be with my sick mother in China was overwhelming. I had to leave my beloved job, a choice that left a scar that seemed as though it would never fully heal.

As I gradually adjusted to a more laid-back retirement life, a life filled with the quiet rhythms of family and self-reflection, an unexpected call shattered my new tranquility. Dr. Yanyu Zhou, the former president of the Edmonton Chinese Writing Club (ECWC), approached me with a proposition that would change the course of my life once again. She asked me to take up the leadership role.

"Why would I do that?" I retorted. I was convinced that my life, in its current state, was a picture of perfection. I saw no need to seek anything further.

But Dr. Zhou's response was like a thunderbolt that pierced through my carefully constructed defenses. "You've got to step out of the small worlds of yourself and your family. There is greater joy out there." Her words hung in the air, resonating deep within me. I was speechless as her message sank in.

Fast forward to the present day, and I am now in my fourth year as the president of the ECWC. It has been a journey filled with countless challenges and triumphs. Together with our enthusiastic members and in collaboration with local organizations, we have achieved something that once seemed like mere dreams. We have organized literary events that have brought the community together, creating a space for the exchange of ideas, stories, and cultures. Our writing workshops have nurtured the talents of emerging writers, helping them find their voices and share their unique perspectives with the world.

Reflecting on my journey as an immigrant in Canada, it has been a voyage of self - discovery, a winding path that has led me through the highs and lows of life. I have learned, through the trials and tribulations, that true happiness is not measured by personal achievements or material possessions. Instead, it is found in the connections we forge with others, in the lives we touch, and in the positive impact we create in the world around us.

As I gaze into the future, I envision endless possibilities— not just for myself but for all the lives that will cross my path along this journey. This chapter of my life serves as a reminder that happiness often emerges from embracing the unknown, from being open-minded enough to redefine our paths when necessary, to discover our strength within, and to realize our support that lies within our community.

The journey is far from over, and while the road ahead may still be fraught with challenges, it is also filled with promise and hope. In time, happiness will find its way to each and every one of us, often in the most unexpected and quiet ways.

# amiskwacîy-wâskahikan
## (ᐊᒥᐣᑳᐧᒋᐊᐧᐣᑲᐦᐃᑲᐣ)

**By Mila Bongco-Philipzig**

amiskwacîy-wâskahikan was not your name
When we first met and I was oh-so-young
And full of dreams  I didn't even realize were not entirely mine
But created, shaped, instilled in me
By people who did not even look like, nor speak like, me


I came as a student, was awestruck by the buildings
The hallowed halls of the university
The imposing professors in tweed suits, woolen coats, and
    leather gloves
And I aspired to be one of them someday.
Until I learned, and learned some more
And wondered why were there gaps, why were there cracks
And why did certain people and voices fall into those gaps and
    cracks
Why was Canada's full history not revealed to me? To many?
Like the Sixties Scoop, and Residential Schools,
And what were those red dresses lining the streets
During the month of May?


amiskwacîy-wâskahikan I honour you
I hear my ancestors voices when I seek to know you
They remind me to learn history from the people and the land
Not just from books edited, maybe even censored, by many
Nothing man-made outlives land's memory.
The land that was always here is the same land that will save us
As my ancestors keep saying
Listen to the land, we and the land are one.

# My Ongoing Journey with Edmonton Chinatown

By Wai-Ling Lennon （姚慧玲）

I MOVED TO CANADA WITH MY FIANCÉ IN APRIL 1983. AFTER A FEW days of farewell celebrations in Hong Kong, we arrived in Edmonton. I was shocked at the quietness of the city. There was no Sunday shopping then, so weekends were slow and sleepy times.

One day, I took the bus to go downtown. I wanted to explore Chinatown. I longed for some familiar scenes, foods, and language to soothe my homesickness. The bus ride was over half an hour. It took me from a residential neighbourhood of bungalows to high rise apartments, to car dealerships, to restaurants and to downtown office buildings. I enjoyed the sight of them all. I was trying to learn about the city.

I got off at a stop on Jasper Avenue and 95 street and walked north. What I saw made me sad. I almost cried! I was used to the hustle and bustle of pedestrians, shops, and markets in Hong Kong. I was expecting the sounds of vendors selling produce and fruits, fish, poultry and other wares. In Hong Kong, I remember the sounds of buses opening and closing doors as riders went on and off, people hurrying, all the chatting, and cars honking – it was all like an unrehearsed orchestra, an organized chaos of people and cars sharing the limited space of Hong Kong island.

Here, I saw shops with doors and windows blocked off. The sidewalks in front of them were dusty. Some stores have Chinese scripts on the wall or on the entrance of the building. The writings were faded. I was surprised. In Hong Kong, an empty space seldom sits for long before it is replaced. So, this scene in front of me was like a photograph in a book or a scene in a movie. There were so many abandoned buildings. My heart sank. I never thought that I would see that kind of desolation in a city known to have an economic boom in the 1970s.

Years passed where I had not visited Chinatown. I was busy pursuing my second degree in Education and started our family. But I was aware of a new Chinese gate called Harbin Gate (中華門) that was opened in October 1987. It is located at the corner of 97 Street and 102 Avenue. In fact, that section (between 97 to 95 Street) of 102 Avenue was titled Harbin Road (哈爾濱路). The gate was built to commemorate the twinning of Edmonton with the City of Harbin in Heilongjiang province of China. I was very proud and happy to see the street name in Chinese script. The gate was beautiful. I felt my Chinese identity had been validated.

After our first daughter was old enough for walks, we visited Chinatown north or Business Chinatown regularly on the weekends. We shopped fresh produce at a grocery store called Tai Fat (泰發). They had fresh vegetables and fruits on tables outside the shop. Inside, we purchased meat and frozen ocean fish, spices, sauces, crackers and cookies. We bought many delicious groceries. I was so excited and energized to see packages of food with Chinese scripts with which I am quite familiar. In the shop I could hear workers and customers speak Cantonese. The sight and the smell reminded me of Hong Kong. Tai Fat was a very busy place and their business was good. A few years later, the store was closed. I was sad and missed that place where I could buy familiar food items and where I could converse with people in Cantonese.

Occasionally, we went to Marco Polo Restaurant for dim sum. We liked it because it was on the second floor of Pacific Rim Mall (now Pacific Mall), and there was a lot of natural light. In the late 1980s, it was new and grand. On the main floor of the mall, there was a St. Hornore's Cake Shop (聖安娜西餅店). They sold western cakes and pastries. The name St. Hornore's was a very famous bakery chain in Hong Kong. I think the owner of this cake shop chose this name to attract customers who were from Hong Kong.

There was a Hong Kong and Shanghai Bank on the main floor of Pacific Mall which was always busy in the 1980s. Jolly Times was a travel agency on the main floor as well. My family booked many flights through them before the system allowed customers to book their own. There was a very friendly lady who assisted us for flights to Hong Kong and India. It was so relaxing to have someone book connected flights for us. Jolly Times served the community until COVID hit and they had to close due to the lack of business. Beside Jolly Times, there was a good Chinese bookstore called Tom Lee (a name of a musical instrument chain in Hong Kong). They carried Chinese newspapers, magazines, children's books, and stationeries such as bamboo brushes and Chinese ink. The owner and the workers were always welcoming.

In the 1980s and 1990s, 97 Street was busy. I was so excited to see shoppers with black hair and brown eyes like me. There were grandparents taking grandchildren to Marco Polo for dim sum. There were mothers taking their children for grocery shopping. Children could point to items that they like, such as Porky, chocolate dipped cracker sticks. Some were happy to pick up haw flakes (dried haw fruit) for snacks. There were so many happy faces because they were with their loved ones.

The familiar sounds of Cantonese were like music to my ears. I was always busy pointing out pictures, Chinese scripts, and other items in the shops to my daughters. Chinatown north had various hair salons, cafes, barbeque shops and herbs stores and even three bookstores. It was an excellent place for me to share Chinese culture with my husband and daughters. Every time I returned home from Chinatown, I felt so charged up, like a battery-operated bunny!

Sadly, the economy in Chinatown deteriorated in the late 1990s and in early 2000. Many immigrants came to Edmonton from Hong Kong to escape unexpected changes as Hong Kong was to be returned to China in 1997. After a few years, the situation in Hong Kong was stable. Many of them were disappointed in the lack of job opportunities here and returned to Hong Kong. Subsequently, the bookstores, gift shops, noodle houses, and restaurants closed one after the other. As the Cantonese-speaking Chinese immigrants left, many businesses could not survive. Every time I saw a store closed, I felt like l had lost a friend. We had less and less choices of shops to visit and places to satisfy our taste buds.

On top of this, the announcement of the construction of the light rail transit line cutting along 102 Avenue devastated the Edmonton Chinese community. There were no public consultations held with residents and businesses in the area. Despite a couple of protests to the City of Edmonton, the project continued. The Harbin Gate was removed on a bitterly cold night in November 2017. There was a posting through social media that there was a goodbye vigil for the gate. It was a very short notice. My husband and I went to join about 50 attendees bidding a tearful farewell to our beloved gate.

By the time we arrived around ten o'clock, the gate had already been cut into three structures, placed side-by-side. There were about 10 to 12 staff from TransEd Valley Line LRT waiting for the vigil to complete so they could carry out the move. I saw the gate's shadow on the south-facing wall of a pharmacy shop. It was tranquil, beautiful and haunting at the same time as if the gate were saying "remember that I once stood here as the landmark that many Edmontonians adored for 20 years".

For the vigil, the Chinese Benevolent Association of Edmonton prepared extra large pink polo shirts for the attendees to put on top of their overcoats. Some people held a candle in their hands. It was a very sad and solemn good-bye. Mrs. Mei Hung spoke about how her late husband Mr. Kim Hung led the Chinese community in fund-raising events for the construction of the gate.

We reminisced about the early 1980s when there were numerous fund-raising banquets and walks for this gate. They were well attended as the Edmonton Chinese community was very excited to welcome a Chinese gate. A symbol of twinning between Edmonton and Harbin of China. The government from the City of Harbin sent expert stonemasons and boxes and boxes of golden yellow tiles. When it was completed many Chinese Edmontonians were so proud to have a physical structure that represents their culture of over 5000 years. The street sign for Harbin Road was also written in Chinese scripts. Years later, I learned from some Chinese seniors who were involved in the project that in Harbin, the road from the airport to the city centre is called Edmonton Boulevard.

Harbin Gate was completed in 1987 and was removed in 2017. It was only twenty years! Gates like that in China and around the world usually stay for centuries and are seldom moved. Many community members were very sad about the removal.

Now, I have lived in Edmonton for 42 years which is twice the time I lived in Hong Kong. Edmonton is my home – my "transplanted roots." I have witnessed many changes in the city. Many have improved the neighbourhoods, and some have not. In a democratic society, citizens are usually invited to voice their opinions on public transportation matters. I feel that the construction of the Valley Line interrupts local foot traffic along 102 Avenue between 95 and 97 Street and I learned from many community leaders that there was no public consultation with the residents in the area at all.

In December 2017, a few local artists gathered at Double Greetings restaurant and shared their grief about the gate. As a result, 哎呀aiya Collective was formed. The group hosted a calligraphy and memories writing event at the Nook Café. The public was invited to write what the gate meant for them. I crocheted about 100 doilies to attach to the paper strips with printing of "中華門". Participants wrote messages on the back of these strips. 哎呀aiya Collective hung them on the metal fence where the gate used to be. The colourful doilies and messages allowed the community to share their feelings about the gate. These personal heartfelt messages were there for at least a year or two. 哎呀aiya Collective was grateful that the City allowed them to stay up for a long time. Many motorists and pedestrians who passed by the area appreciated them.

In the following years, a few young artists and community activist groups have emerged. They have a common mission – to bring back the vibrancy that Chinatown once had. Given the economic times and drug crises in the area, Chinatown is experiencing indescribable hardship. Many community members are struggling to understand how our beloved neighbourhood makes visitors uncomfortable. The groups collaborate with each other, and with their strengths and talents, they are making a difference.

Chinatown Greetings was headed by two artists who encouraged other artists to carry out projects to attract Edmontonians to Chinatown. The first year they sponsored Ray Day Lam, a visual artist to design posters that reflect Chinese festivals. The second year they sponsored Jordon Hon, a lens-based photographer to coordinate "Untouchable Chinatown." The project included a photo exhibition from eleven community members and their writings. A limited number of *Untouchable Chinatown* photos and writings were printed for fund-raising. The surplus will be used for the following year to sponsor another artist to plan and conduct a project related to Chinatown revitalization.

Re:VITA, a group of young people, held "Chinatown After Dark" gatherings to invite people to Chinatown and enjoy delicious foods, play mahjong, sing karaoke, view special cars and so on. A short back-alley way between 97 and 98 Street was filled with different booths and vendors. The gatherings were fun and welcoming. The name Re:VITA is a short form for the term "revitalization." They organized year-round clean-ups in Chinatown north on every second Saturday of the month. Volunteers sign up through their social media postings. These clean-ups are usually led by William Lau and Andrew Hui, members of Re:VITA. In winter they even shovel and sprinkle sand on the sidewalks. I am very proud of what this group has done to bring positive energy to the neighbourhood. Presently, the clean-up group is funded by Reach Edmonton. After the clean-up, the group of volunteers of diverse backgrounds would share their experiences and ideas over lunch. They would talk about what they could do to help revitalize Chinatown and the neighbourhood. I learned that "Chinatown After Dark" is in fact, one of the results of many friendly and caring conversations.

Emily Chu, a visual artist organized a "Togather - Art Fair Market" held in Edmonton Chinatown Multicultural Centre. The markets, held in 2024 and 2025 around lunar new year, were well attended. Many visitors were amazed by the variety of booths and food vendors at the market. Some commented that they did not know such a cultural centre exists. Chu led another project "Chinatown Stories Map" in 2024 and provided information on parks, murals, and shops with interesting stories about each of them. The map was translated in Vietnamese and Chinese (traditional script). For the Year of The Snake, Chu collaborated with the Edmonton Oilers and designed an Edmonton Oilers logo for the year. The designs are so well designed that they reflect the essence of the Oilers' logo and the Chinese New Year culture. The proceeds will go to support future projects led by Re:VITA.

Edmonton has many clan associations such as: Gees, Wongs, Yees, Lees, Mahs etc. They have a long history of helping their compatriots since the first Chinese John Gee (朱忠孝) arrived in Edmonton in 1892. On the Chinese New Year's Day of Year of The Dragon (2024) the Mah Society of Edmonton opened "The Journey of Mah" exhibits at their society which is located on 101A Avenue and between 96 and 97 Street. The exhibit not only documents the arrival of people with Mah as last name but also shares the general history of Chinese arrival in Edmonton from over a hundred years ago. There are stories about adaptation and courage of many of our seniors in the city. It is professionally organized and presents what no clan society has ever accomplished.

Chinatown now has two guardian angels painted by Branden Cha, a mural artist. One is the White Tiger facing west on the back wall of Marble Restaurant on 97 Street and 106 Avenue. The second one is the Azure Dragon facing east on the side wall of Edmonton Mah Society on 101A Avenue between 96 and 97 Street. Both murals have a poem written by Chinatown artivists William Lau and Catherine Wang. The poems urge the guardian angels to protect Edmonton Chinatown and nearby neighbourhoods. I know there will be three more guardians planned: the Black Tortoise, the Vermilion Bird, and the Thunderbird. The Thunderbird is specifically to honour the land that we are on – the Indigenous Land where many nations of Indigenous peoples live, work and travel through for centuries. I look forward to seeing them when they are completed.

In 2024, 哎呀aiya Collective also supported a project titled "Chinatown Care Package – a Series of Wellness Workshops.". There were 12 workshops related to wellness. The variety included: Peace Making Circle, Common Chinese Herb Soups, Poetry Writing, Vansu (dumplings) Making, Calligraphy, Acupuncture, Mindfulness, Chinese Sponge Cake Making, To Draw over Dim Sum, Incense Making and Our Tree of Care. The main goal of these workshops is to promote healthy living for the body and the mind. These workshops provided a safe place for many attendees to learn and connect. From the positive feedback collected, the organizers know that their goals of promoting wellness have been achieved. I was involved in this series of workshops and earned myself a new title "Auntie Wai-Ling" which I love!

I have retired from teaching for a few years now. I am honoured to have been invited to help with various community projects. I have shared Chinese culture with many people and in return I have learned from many community leaders about their contributions to Edmonton. I have met many kind individuals who are full of energy and ideas. I hope that with what I know and what I can offer could inspire more community members to get involved and work with these young professionals and artists. I am certain that they know "Auntie Wai-Ling" will always cheer them on! I look forward to seeing many creative and revitalizing projects take place in years to come.

# Where Are You, China Gate?[2]

## By William Wang

Across from yesterday's Coliseum, the old hockey place,
Here is a fenced storage, a lock on the iron gate.
Scattered, with sand, gravel, and snowflakes......
Is that you, China Gate?

Wires and barriers,
Obscuring the golden tile's former glory.
Snow and frost,
Covering the double dragons' prosperous play.
Morning bell, no longer tolls,
Evening drum, no longer beats.
Sawed off shoulders,
There lies the exposed chest.
Are the stone lions in the vicinity trying to communicate?
Is the Chinese red greeting fading?

To remember Bethune's rescue to victory,
To cherish the sisterhood, connecting to Canadian mate,
Harbin traveled thousands of miles to donate,
A nation's appreciation was built on the "Close Friendship
    Gate."
Farthest Edmonton became Harbin's closest thoughts,
The Harbin Gate became the world's northernmost China
    Gate!

---

2    November 4, 2017, Edmonton China gate was taken down for
     LRT construction, this gift from China to Edmonton has been
     in the city storage since.

Raymond Keung, "Harbin Gate" Watercolour 2025

Expanding the city's light railway,
Taking down the China Gate,
Nowhere to relocate this fate,
No reopening date to celebrate,
 "The gate is too narrow......"
 "97th Street is too wide......"
Either bureaucracy excuses are too hasty,
Or 97th Street is too easy to manipulate.

China Gate stood tall to motivate,
China Gate stayed open to tolerate.
Welcome people who came early or came late,
Marked this place to accept people to stay or retreat.
Little luck is found in the fortune cookie this winter day,
Good "Feng Shui" seems to have left 97th street.
Chinatown is now incomplete without its gate
Thirty years of blessings now lie in wait.

Despite Harper's apologies to Chinese railway workers being a
    century late,
Our nation moves forward to a multicultural path, to
    collaborate.
There are Totem Poles, Mosques, and Cathedrals......
But where are you, China Gate?
Restore the gate,
The faith innate.

# Tatming: An Enlightened and Sagacious Chinese in Edmonton[3]

**By Yuzhen Li**

SHORTLY AFTER I ARRIVED IN EDMONTON, I NOTICED THE CHINESE name Yee Tatming 余達明 since his calligraphy and painting works were posted in the Edmonton Chinatown Chinese Library and all Chinese restaurants that I visited. Calligraphy and traditional Chinese painting are pure Chinese art forms. Hence, for me, a Chinese woman with a passion for Chinese culture, I was deeply touched by his name in a foreign land. Later, I read several articles published by him in the local Chinese newspapers. All of these indicated that he was quite an influential figure in Edmonton.

Finally, I had the chance to meet him in person. I always felt that it was meant to be. On a sunny summer day, Jiani嘉妮, the librarian in the Chinese library, invited Mr. Yee to meet with me and my husband in the library. Mr. Yee looked very much like a painter, I thought — tall and strong build, with a well-proportioned face, kind and clear eyes, and particularly the broad forehead, which, like a drawing board, left a large room for imagination. Yet, his well-defined lips, like the gate to a closed treasure house, seemed to hold rich and inexhaustible treasures. For this, I believed that he also possessed the essence of a writer.

---

3    This essay was originally written in Chinese by Li Yuzhen 李玉真 and translated into English by Rong Guo 国荣, with abridgment. Tatming, the first name of Yee Tatming 余達明, literally means "open-minded, wise and intelligent; arriving at the high level of enlightenment".

The rows of bookshelves and the aroma of books created a very good atmosphere for communication. With a cup of tea in hand, we talked and talked, from painting and calligraphy to literature, from the experience of immigration to feelings of reminiscence. I admired Mr. Yee in silence for his broad and solid knowledge and the wealth of experience, a true treasure in his heart. I could not help but exclaim, "Is there anything more joyful than making a new friend on the same wavelength?"

Later, I read his essay published in the local newspaper, 红豆汤圆(Red Bean Rice Ball), which won him a Bing Xin Literature Prize. It was based on his experience of eating red bean rice ball on three different occasions with his adopted mother, who shed tears each time. The essay described the deep relationship between a mother and a son, highlighting the images of a mother inspiring reverence and a son being affectionate and grateful in return. The writing is fluent and spirited, imbued with deep emotions and profound meaning. Through the essay, I learned more about Mr. Yee's life trajectory and his rich inner world. Deeply touched, I authored an article to respond, 红豆的另一种相思 (A Different Longing of the Red Bean), which was published in *The Chinese Journal* (《光华报》).

Mr. Yee was born during the second Sino-Japanese War and suffered hardships from an early age. He was taken in by an orphanage in Hong Kong. At the age of 12, he was adopted by his foster mother. Under his foster mother's careful nurturing, he completed his higher education and graduated from the Department of Fine Arts at the Chinese Culture University in Taiwan.

In the essay, he describes his first impression of his foster mother, who is "nearly sixty years old at the time. Tall and slender, with a straight back and not a hint of obesity. Wearing a gray-blue cheongsam, with her thick black hair neatly combed back, she carries a black bag on her arm, and her oval face is lit up by a gentle smile." Mr. Yee mentions several times her "straight back" and "gentle smile."

His foster mother was diagnosed with cancer when she was 93 years old. She said to the doctor, he wrote, "It's very simple actually. Instead of treating this cancer as an enemy, I regard it as a guest, an unwelcome guest living inside me. Now that I cannot drive it away, I had better treat it well, ... make it feel at home. Let it live its way, and I live mine. We two live harmoniously. No invasion, nor violation. We thrive together. Ha ha ha...."

Like wielding a brush in painting, Mr. Yee sketches out with just a few strokes his foster mother's strong and optimistic character and her shining qualities. This kind, upright, and knowledgeable woman deeply affects Mr. Yee and influences him his whole life.

Even in his octogenarian years, Mr. Yee still remembers his mother's kindness and teachings. Once at a coffeehouse, he mentions again his foster mother. He says: "My mother once told me that the reason people are respected as the noblest of all creatures is not because they can accumulate material possessions, but because they can overcome the misfortunes that fate imposes and challenge the fate! One must be kind and loving. Without action, the so-called kindness and love are meaningless." It is exactly because of his foster mother's influence that Mr. Yee is a diligent, determined, kind, and loving man.

Mr. Yee once worked in Hong Kong, East Africa, and other places. In 1975, he immigrated to Canada and settled down in Edmonton, Alberta. He worked at many things including architectural designer and university lecturer. He established his own studio to teach both Chinese and Western painting and held personal and group exhibitions. Amy Lau, the famous Chinese writer living in Edmonton, once studied painting with Mr. Yee. In her book, 驀然回首看愛城 (*Looking back: My Seven Years in Edmonton*), she writes, "Mr. Yee has a profound understanding of both ancient and modern art. He possesses noble artistic cultivation and integrity. ... With humor, he explains principles of painting, and in light-hearted conversations, he teaches painting techniques. ... Students not only gain insights into painting skills and calligraphy methods but also enhance their personal artistic cultivation."

Mr. Yee also engaged in literary creation and teaching. For over two decades, he has served as a columnist for the *Edmonton Chinese News* (愛華報) and the *Chinese Journal* (光華報) in Edmonton. He has also been the host of the "Cultural Lecture" on the Chinese radio station. Mr. Yee integrated his great love into his teaching, imparting knowledge with warmth and dedication.

I once attended Mr. Yee's lecture about literature and authored a report on behalf of the Edmonton Chinese Writing Club. The title is "Life and the First-Hand Materials of Literary Creation." As a well-established painter and writer in Edmonton, Mr. Yee possesses rich artistic sensibilities and creative experiences. He applied his painting techniques to writing, interweaving the virtual and the real with moderate embellishment, and fully revealed the relationship between life and the first-hand materials. He also taught the methods of collecting materials and their value orientation. His interaction with the audience made the lecture both profound and engaging.

Mr. Yee believed that life is the most important source for literary creation, for example, family, love, life, and death. Each person's experience is unique, and that uniqueness is the wonderful and authentic source. Many literary works are unsuccessful because of their selection of first-hand materials. Topics that are too old and lack novelty are boring. This is related to the author's limited ability to select authentic life experiences and their comparatively shallow understanding of life. Drawing on traditional Chinese culture and Western rational and emotional knowledge, Mr. Yee wrote out particularly the following three groups of characters: 天(heaven), 人(human), 地(earth); 心(heart), 人, 物(object), 知(knowledge), 感(sensation); 人, 天使(angel), 魔鬼(devil), etc., to illustrate his understanding and perception of the world.

Mr. Yee concluded by emphasizing the importance of ethics in collecting first-hand materials. He stated that one could not steal others' materials, nor write about others' private affairs without permission. We seek materials in order to write, but what is literature for? He asked. It is for love, he responds, the love of people, the love of freedom, and the love of peace. Most importantly, he added, writing should be done with a heart full of love; only then could one produce works with eternal value.

In the summer of 2013, knowing that I was about to leave Edmonton, Mr. Yee prepared for me a piece of calligraphy, a poem he produced especially for me, with his seals stamped on it. A Chinese friend exclaimed, "Wow, what a precious gift! In Edmonton, people usually pay him 100 Canadian dollars for one character." I brought it back to Beijing, framed and hung it in our living room. Whenever I see it, I think very fondly of Mr. Yee.

Our communications continue even today. He sent to me his autobiographical novel, 珍珠串 (*The String of Pearls*), which presents stories of his legendary life. He uses a string of pearls as a metaphor to describe each person he met and he is grateful to. He inscribed his gratitude on the book cover: "Without love, there is nothing left in our life." Communicating with him is always inspiring and comes from the deep bottom of our hearts. Here is an example, a message he sent in WeChat:

A person's conscience and moral awareness together form a flower of the soul, which can be put simply as a "heart flower." The fragrance emitted from the heart flower is the charm of one's personality. The eternal value and the hope of the human being come entirely from a mature and good-hearted spirit. Only those who, with an upright and compassionate heart, have the wisdom of judging right and wrong, be good at reflecting and observing one's own thoughts and behavior, seeing others as oneself ... could emanate the charm of personality, and make people feel like the spring breeze touching their face when interacting with others.

This is exactly how I feel when communicating with him — the spring breeze touching my face.

On September 17, 2024, Mr. Yee sent me a message that the municipal government of Edmonton held a grand opening ceremony for his calligraphy for the Chinese archway. Over four hundred people attended the event. Above the red Chinese archway, there are four golden characters on a black horizontal plaque, 天下为公, which looked so powerful, with a grand and imposing aura. The quote, from礼记 (*The Book of Rites*), was taken by Sun Yat-sen, the builder of the Republic of China, as a political ideal, and it was engraved and passed down until today. Mr. Yee wrote down these four characters, which revealed, to some extent, his political vision — to treat the whole world as one community.

**Photo provided by Rong Guo**

Just as his name, 達明, indicates, Mr. Yee has been striving for his whole life in order to arrive at the other bank of enlightenment. I once wrote him a seven-character acrostic to celebrate his eightieth birthday in 2019. The poem, embedded with his literary works and names he once used in the past, summarized my understanding of his eighty years' vicissitudes and attainments, and expressed my sincere blessing for his future:

致志丹青江长流，
余霞催波弄扁舟；
达观神韵妙笔挥，
明慧情真佳文留；
八斗通古串珍珠，
十分融今说红豆；
寿桃仙境仁者寿，
诞辰春生乐悠悠！

Dedicated to the endless art of painting like the flowing river,
The evening glow stirs the ripples to play with a solitary boat;
With a broad view and divine charm, the wonderful brush
    moves freely,
With wise and sincere emotion, done with beautiful articles;
The pearls were strung with wisdom of past and present,
Even the red beans are very much in harmony with the now.
In the fairyland of longevity peach, the benevolent lives long,
Along with the coming of spring, birthday brings long-lasting
    delight!

Sheila C, "Winter" Watercolour 2024

## Thank you to the Authors

We are thankful to the authors who shared their words of courage, love, and dreams in this anthology. May we continue to connect and help shape the future of our communities and our city.

# About the Authors

**CANDICE JOY OLIVA** (she/they/siya) is an immigrant settler from Bicol, Philippines to Amiskwacîwâskahikan on Treaty 6. Siya hopes these heritage poems will carry her 2022-24 memories with kapwa at the Edmonton Urban Farm— from gardening with the Newcomer Centre, to launching their debut chapbook ISARO. *"It is a joyful honour to be known and be loved by kapwa on this land I have grown to love too."* IG: @candicejoyoliva.

**CYNTHIA PALMARIA** migrated from the Philippines to Montreal in 1987. She graduated from University of Waterloo with a Bachelor's in Science, graduate studies in Leadership in Healthcare, Masters in Intercultural and International Communication at Royal Roads University. Cynthia works as a Faculty for the Radiation Therapy Program at the University of Alberta. She was one of the founding members of Migrante-Alberta, a Filipino organization advocating for the rights and welfare of workers.

**DAN LI** Previously taught mathematics at a university in Beijing. She currently works as a software engineer. She started writing poetry in February 2024 and states *"In my eyes, everything can be a poem. I am grateful for everyone in my life, and everything I encounter."*

**EMILY TWOREK** is an Alberta-born creator with a passion for digital media and storytelling. Holding a degree in Animation and Visual Effects, she brings a unique visual perspective to her writing. She draws inspiration from family, friends, and past experience working in the oil and gas industry in Alberta. When not working on animation projects, she enjoys reading, studying languages, and spending time with her husband and two cats.

**GOLDWIN (Gold) MCEWEN:** a western Canadian author and publisher. Develops professional communications, bilingual children's picture books, and publishes poetry and short stories. Winner of an IABC Capital Award of Excellence in Communications Skills and Tactics. I'm very excited to be co-authoring a book as well as producing a play for Vancouver's Fringe this year.

**JESUS TIGULO** is a Filipino immigrant, now living in Edmonton with his loving wife of 33 years, a son, and two daughters, all still together under one roof. Jesus has a Bachelor of Arts from the Philippines. In his early years, he was an active participant of youth activism that advocated for social justice and advancement of nationalist movement.

*"One's life can be an endless struggle but with God, nothing is impossible."*

**KHRYSTYNA ZALUTSKA** was born in Ivano-Frankivsk, Ukraine, and later raised in Canada. She studies politics and English at the University of Alberta, exploring what the academic field has to offer. Khrystyna balances her time coaching skiing, hiking, and studying.

*"My passion for literature, politics, and outdoor adventures shapes my perspective on the world."*

**LAUNA-RAE LINAKER,** PhD candidate, is an educator and researcher exploring care theory, narrative inquiry, and somatic autobiographical inquiry. She holds space for women to journey through somatic and autobiographical inquiry, unravelling deeply embedded narratives and patterns that have shaped their sense of self. Through this process, they awaken to the wisdom of their body and story, realigning with their inherent sovereignty and cultivating an unshakable trust in their own authority.

**MANNA LIU** immigrated to Canada with her family in 2003. She was a librarian in China. She now creates stories about the hardships of first-generation Chinese immigrants aspiring for better lives. Her books have won prizes and have been published in North America. Her new book *One Person's Dance* was published in Chinese in 2024, and the English translation will be out in 2025.

**MARVIN CAO** is an engineer who loves writing and reading, especially fiction. He admires Gabriel García Márquez and Milan Kundera's novels and enjoys non-fiction by Peter Hessler and Svetlana Alexievich. Balancing technical work with literary exploration, Marvin finds inspiration in the profound narratives of both imagined and real worlds.

**MILA BONGCO-PHILIPZIG** is a writer, visual artist, and community organizer. Her children's books, poems, essays and podcasts have been published in Canada, USA, the Philippines, and Germany. The diaspora of the global majority is a recurring theme in her writings. She is an avid advocate for human rights and social justice.

*What is the point of art if not to resist?*

www.milabongco.com
IG: @milabillabong
FB: Mila Bongco

**OLIVER ROSSIER** has a BA in History and Political Science, and an MA in Communications and Technology, both from University of Alberta. "The Art of Uli" is his first attempt to create narrative non-fiction. Oliver has helped bring several social transformation initiatives to Edmonton, including: Hold These Truths; Principles of Resistance: the Gordon Hirabayashi Story; and the Pan-African Symposium.

**PAUL FUJISHIGE** was born Winnipeg and moved to Alberta in 1980. He held various positions in the government, not-for-profit, and education sectors. His primary work was with people with disabilities. He continues to advocate and promote the rights of all citizens.

Paul is a sansei (3rd generation Japanese Canadian), re-discovering his roots, including learning more about his family history in Canada and Japan. Paul is past President of the Edmonton Japanese Community Association.

**PRAVATIKA RAI TAMANG** originated from Nepal and came to Edmonton in 2019. She is actively involved in her cultural community and continuously contributes to building strong communities in general by working at Action for Healthy Communities as well as volunteering at the We and the World

Centre, International Heritage & Language Association, among other community work.

**RONG GUO (国荣)** currently teaches at China University of Mining & Technology, Beijing. She translated from English to Chinese Momme Brodersen's *Walter Benjamin: A Biography*, J. Hillis Miller's *An Innocent Abroad: Lectures in China*, and Ugo Rossi's *Cities in Global Capitalism*. Her main interests are post-colonial theories, diasporic studies and overseas Chinese literature; *Approaching History: The Fictional Worlds of Ha Jin and Yan Geling* is her English book published in 2018.

**ROXANNE RIEMER** is a proud mother of two wonderful daughters who keep her busy and bring her endless joy. In her free time, Roxanne enjoys crafting and rollerblading with her daughters and unwinding with a good puzzle. Through the Edmonton Chinese Writing Club, she has discovered writing as a path to self-exploration and healing. *"The only real failure is never trying."*

**RYAN LACANILAO** (IG: @ooakosiryan) is a sometimes poet, sometimes podcaster (@whatsthetsismis), and sometimes musician (@thecalamansiclub) living in McCauley. He's published in both English and Kapampangan, and you can find his writing in *The Polyglot, Hungry Zine, Everything Is Urgent*, and elsewhere. He's currently writing a book of letters to his 4-year-old son.

**TING PIMENTEL-ELGER's** body of work represents diversity and multifariousness, intermixture of words, images, languages, cultural traditions and a variety of innovation and invention and tons of fun. She embraces diversity, equity, inclusion and is a certified trauma-informed Yoga instructor.

*Ang hindi marunong magmahal sa sariling wika, masahol pa sa hayop o malansang isda.* A quote from Dr. Jose Rizal, Philippines' national hero, writer, poet, and polymath.

**WAI-LING LENNON (**姚慧玲**)** moved to Edmonton from Hong Kong in 1983. She was a teacher with Edmonton Public Schools for 25 years. After she retired from teaching, she completed an oral history project with Edmonton Chinese Library Foundation. For the last few years, she has been a member of aiya 哎呀 Collective and took part in various community events related to the revitalization of the Edmonton Chinatown area.

**WILLIAM WANG** dedicated 23 years to the City of Edmonton as a Transit Bus Operator/Auxiliary Instructor. He received the 2010 Canadian Urban Transit Association Outstanding Achievement Award, nominated for the City Manager's Award, and Safe Driving/Perfect Attendance Awards.

His English poetry and artwork have been featured in *Edmonton Transit News, ETS on the Move, Deputy City Manager's Update.* His artwork has been included in the City Ambassadors training manual.

**YANJIAN (George) LUO** served as a senior engineer at a design research institute in Shanghai, specializing in the design and consulting of metro systems, urban tunnels, and geotechnical pit engineering. He has published over forty scientific papers and translations in academic journals. Currently, he is a member of the Edmonton Chinese Writers Club (ECWC). He is passionate about exploring new opportunities and connecting with people from diverse backgrounds.

**YING (Cathy) SHI** earned her Canadian doctorate in ESL Teacher Education. She advocates for student and immigrant empowerment. Her research primarily focuses on the career development of internationally trained immigrants and children global citizenship education. After 35 years of teaching in ESL, she reflects on her cross-cultural experiences through writing and leads the Edmonton Chinese Writing Club, an inclusive organization dedicated to promoting multiculturalism through the transformative power of words.

**YUZHEN LI (李玉真),** a member of the Edmonton Chinese Writing Club, was once the deputy editor-in-chief of the literary magazine, 敦煌 (*Dunhuang*). She has published more than ten books, and her works appear in various publications in China, Canada, Australia, and other countries. She also received numerous literary awards, including an award for lyric creation. 西部女人(Women in the West) is one of her most widely circulated works.

**Aaron Harvey, "Fishing Grizzly"**

# About The Nina Haggerty Centre

The Nina Haggerty Centre for the Arts (the Nina) is an art studio and gallery in Edmonton, Alberta where artists with developmental and other disabilities create and share their work.

Over 200 artists make up the Nina Collective, working in painting, drawing, printmaking, ceramics, textiles, and more.

We believe that all people have the right to achieve their highest potential, which includes the right to creative expression, and are committed to providing artistic opportunities for artists who face barriers.

Facebook: Nina Haggerty Centre for the Arts
Instagram: @ninahaggertyarts
Twitter: @ninahaggertyart

Jared Quinney, "Raven in the River Valley" 2022

# Acknowledgements

We are truly grateful to all the contributors – for their courage in sharing their stories and their trust in us and this book project. We extend utmost thanks to: Cathy Shi, President, Edmonton Chinese Writing Club (EWCW); the project coordinators: Roxanne Riemer, Ting Pimentel-Elger, and Mila Bongco-Philipzig; editing assistance from Goldwin McEwen and Rong Guo; cover art and section page artist, Eoshanelle Francisco; Kate Boorman for the writing sessions; Dr. Olenka Bilash for advice on ethics and protecting identities; Janice Easton, Director of Communications & Artistic Outreach at The Nina for facilitating the use of artworks; the various artists at the Nina Haggerty Centre; and to Oliver Rossier for suggesting the collaboration with The Nina.

Thank you for graciously sharing all your talents.

We also wish to acknowledge the Edmonton Heritage Council for funding this project and supporting our vision to gather stories from various cultural communities in Edmonton and make these accessible to the public.

Last but not least, we are extremely grateful to be able to live and work on this land. Edmonton – Amiskwaciwâskahikan – is located within Treaty 6 Territory, original home to many diverse groups of Indigenous peoples including the nêhiyawak (Cree), Denesuline (Dene), Niitsitapi (Blackfoot), Anishinaabe (Saulteaux), Nakota Sioux (Stoney), Inuit and Métis. We are grateful that we are able to honor and practice our cultures and build our homes on this land. We pay homage to all caretakers of this land – past, present, and future – and commit to careful and considerate use of resources, so that there will be land, water, and abundance for our neighbours as well as people in the future.

Eli Abada, "Star" Acrylic and coloured pencil

# Thank you to the Artists

Thank you to the following artists whose creativity and talents added the pops of colours to liven up this book.

All of the artists below are with The Nina Haggerty Centre for Arts, and you can find more information about each one at https://www.thenina.ca/our-artists/.

The one artist not with The Nina is Eoshanelle Francisco. She is a graphic designer and illustrator, originally from the Philippines (https://eoshanellegraphics.myportfolio.com/).

Aaron Harvey
Amynah Pirani
Eli Abada
Eoshanelle Francisco
Jamie Laventure
Jared Quinney
Randy Stennes
Raymond Keung
Sheila C
Ulrike Rossier

Thank you for completing *Edmonton Heritage Stories.*

*We would love if you could help by posting a review at your book retailer and on the PageMaster Publishing site. It only takes a minute and it would really help others by giving them an idea of your experience.*

Thanks

PM Store Author's QR Code
https://pagemasterpublishing.ca/by/
edmonton-chinese-writing-club//

To order more copies of this book, find books by other Canadian authors, or make inquiries about publishing your own book, contact PageMaster at:

PageMaster Publication Services Inc.
11340-120 Street, Edmonton, AB  T5G 0W5
books@pagemaster.ca
**780-425-9303**

catalogue and e-commerce store
**PageMasterPublishing.ca/Shop**

www.ingramcontent.com/pod-product-compliance
Lightning Source LLC
Chambersburg PA
CBHW071346250626
47159CB00004B/1622